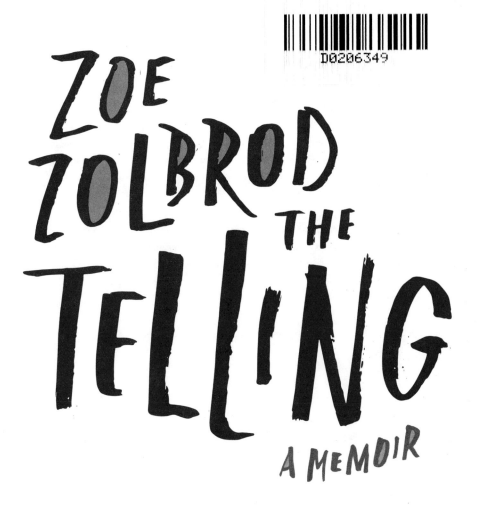

ZOE ZOLBROD

THE TELLING

A MEMOIR

CHICAGO INDEPENDENT PUBLISHING

CURBSIDE SPLENDOR PUBLISHING

AUTHOR'S NOTE:
This is a work of nonfiction based on recollections going back to an early age. Where possible, I've corroborated my memories with journal entries. Dialogue is approximate and appears in quotation marks for the ease of the reader. Aside from all names and some identifying details, which have been changed to protect people's privacy, this book is true to my experience as I recorded and recall it.

Published by Curbside Splendor Publishing, Inc., Chicago, Illinois in 2016.

First Edition
Copyright © 2016 by Zoe Zolbrod
Library of Congress Control Number: 2015948130

ISBN 9781940430744
Edited by Naomi Huffman
Cover image by Mark DeBernardi
Author photo by Elizabeth McQuern
Designed by Alban Fischer

Manufactured in the United States of America.

WWW.CURBSIDESPLENDOR.COM

TO MY CHILDREN
AND THE OTHER CHILDREN
AND EVERYONE WHO HAS BEEN A CHILD

CONTENTS

Prologue 11

PART ONE: YOUTH
The First Time 19
Over the Oceans and Through the Woods 27
The Whole Hot Summer 35
Bounce Babe 45
Mama Bear 49
Girl on the Road 55
Research Shows: Not Just Girls 61
The Visitor's Spot 65
The Second Time 69
The Chauffeur 73
Research Shows: One out of Five 81
Forbearing the Muck 83
Negotiation 91
The End of the Continent 95

PART TWO: ADULTHOOD

Double-Edged Sword 107

Thick Walls 117

Frayed by Tears 123

The Third Time 133

Research Shows: Why It's Hard to Tell 145

The Crooked Little House 149

Indecision 155

The Envy of Others 163

Telling my Parents 169

PART THREE: FAMILY

Butterfly Stories 179

Pocket Knives 185

What Should You Tell? 193

A New Kind of Sense 201

Research Shows: Causes of Pedophilia 207

Shifting Statutes 211

Nice to Meet You 221

Telling a Therapist 227

Asking 233

A Well-Reasoned Argument 241

Telling My Dad 247

Sources 253

Acknowledgments 255

*"What matters in life is not what happens to you
but what you remember and how you remember it."*

—GABRIEL GARCÍA MÁRQUEZ

I got an extra month of maternity leave when my first child was born, and before I went back to work and Anthony quit his job to stay home with our son, we flew to Albuquerque to visit my family.

In the photos from that trip, my shirt is a collage of wet spots of indiscriminate origin. My baby and I were a sloshing pair, our fluids still intertwined. His incessant screaming and crying did not yet yield tears, but it made us both sweat, and my breasts spurted and leaked, and he was plump and a profuse drooler. After a hard few months with a distressed infant, I found it a pleasure to be in dry, sunny New Mexico where at least liquid evaporated quickly and where there were people who shared our awe for the baby. My parents had been divorced for about a dozen years, but they came together to coo at their grandson. Being in the same room with the two of them eased an ache I hadn't allowed myself to acknowledge. Anthony and I even felt confident enough to go to a movie alone, to make a visit to an adjoining town.

Mostly, though, our days were quiet, structured around our son's fledgling sleep schedule. At naptimes, a hush fell over everything. My mom's house was on the newer side of town, in a development built on a hill, each street sitting above the other so as to maximize views of the Sangra de Cristo mountains to the east. The living room section of her first floor was two stories high, with tall windows and skylights. That's where we sat during one naptime toward the end of the visit, going through the bags and bins of baby clothes that my mom had collected from clearance sales and second-hand stores. We knelt on the Berber carpeting and sorted the little jackets and jeans and sleepers into piles—*yes, no, now, later, to return, to resell.*

"So did you hear about Toshi?" she asked me.

The name of my older cousin sent a hot shock through my body. I hadn't heard it spoken out loud in seven years, since I'd told my parents that he'd sexually abused me during the time he'd lived with us as a teenager. After a few stumbling conversations back then, neither my mom nor my dad had mentioned it again, and I'd ceased talking specifically of Toshi to anyone. I stared at the teddy bear face embroidered on the onesie in my hand and braced myself. "Hear what?"

"He's been charged with molesting a girl." She paused. "Or maybe there was more than one. Two?"

I saw an obliterating brightness before I fully understood what she had said, but then: "Oh my God."

What I recall feeling first was a stomach-plunging sense of clarity, almost vindication. Hoisted up from the depths of my mind was the bundle of questions that had dogged me on and off all my life, and here was some kind of answer: what he had done to me was serious. It fit a pattern; it made a horrible kind of sense. But then guilt washed over me. Articulated thoughts would come later, in the hours and weeks and months to come, but the guilt flooded in immediately.

I had not stopped him.

I had not said anything when he was young enough to change course, and so it had gone on. He was now a full-fledged adult, a middle-aged man, and was still molesting children. After years of figuring Toshi had likely used me out of horny desperation to practice for pubescent girls, I switched to a frantic conviction that there was a trail of victims in his wake. That he was a pedophile.

"I'm surprised your dad didn't tell you. He's the one who told me."

I took this as a dig at my father and bristled, even as I absorbed the slap of the fact: he'd said nothing.

"When did it happen?" I strove to keep my voice level.

"I don't know exactly. A while ago. I guess it's taken a long time to go to trial. It's not clear that he did it."

"Of course he did it! Mom! He did it to me!"

"I know. It's awful. It's really awful." Her brow crinkled; she looked sad and vulnerable. Whenever I hugged her I was always surprised at how small she felt. Smaller than me.

I continued with my task. *Sort. Fold. Store. Sort. Fold. Store. Size 2T. Size 3T. Size 4.*

"I'm surprised your dad didn't tell you, but he probably feels guilty. He always felt so guilty about Toshi, because he helped kidnap him from his mom."

"*What?*" Another burst of annihilating white light. My story about myself—my *stories*, any of them, the new one just forming—was shattered.

"How did it go? Oh, I have no memory. Morris and his wife were already separated, and maybe divorced. And he asked Dad to go over to her place and take him? Or they both did it one night. I can't remember. But I think he always felt guilty about that."

"*What?* How old was Toshi?" My voice was ragged.

"Well, was he two or three? Or wait, it had to be after Haruna was born, so older. I think Morris already had Haruna somehow, even though she was just a baby, and now they were going in for Toshi?"

"Then he would have been about five." The same age I turned during the year he'd spent sneaking into my bedroom.

"I can hardly remember anything about it. Oh, I have no memory!"

I have no memory. It was a phrase she said often—usually declaratively, definitively, but right now quite plaintively—all through my life.

My memory, on the other hand, was strong.

"Was this when Morris was living in New York?"

But she had nothing else to give me. She'd told me all she knew.

"Would you mind folding the rest of these?" I asked her. "I want to go lie down."

MY MOTHER'S PRETTY HOUSE was also small and somewhat flimsy. The railing on the open stairway wobbled slightly. The hollow-core doors had no heft, so opening the one to the guest room was like moving a slab of felt. The room was almost entirely taken up by the pull-out bed on which Anthony and the baby lay sleeping. I didn't want to touch or talk to Anthony, or any adult. I wanted to wrap my body around my son, who lay on his belly with his knees tucked under him, his back hunched. I perched on the edge of the bed so as not to disturb him and waited for him to wake.

The sight of his sleep-flushed cheeks and pursed little lips soothed my heart for a moment, but even this joy was painful. My skin hurt from loving him. My breasts ached and pulled toward him; it'd been almost three hours since he'd nursed. Through the rest of my body ran a pulsating siren of panic, some mix of abandonment and rage and grief and guilt and utter confusion that I could hardly bear. The stuffy room, the silent house, and all this roar of emotion.

Oh my baby. Oh my baby. Wake up. Wake up.

And then his tiny face scrunched, his arm shot out and his butt lifted. He gave one mewing cry, and I gathered him to me and lifted my shirt. His body softened into mine and my milk came down with a narcotic rush. I felt almost histrionically sanctimonious. I was a mother. I was feeding my child. He was safe in my arms.

And then:

If I had told I could have saved that girl.

I did tell.

It wasn't soon enough. It wasn't loud enough.

I was a child, too. It's not my fault.

No one said it was.

I conjured an image of Toshi as a befuddled, stick-limbed boy being hustled out of a basement apartment in the dead of a warm autumn night. *His mother! He's going to need his mother!* Was I more worried for that boy or for the girl or for myself or for the baby in my arms who embodied the vulnerability of us all?

Abandonment stunned me again, and the rootedness of nursing began to feel like a burden. I was trapped on the bed when I wanted to twitch away, to run, walk for miles, to leave this family behind and lick my wounds in private, make of them something else. But I couldn't.

The baby's sucking slowed to a nibble. He dozed; I sat, stuck, roiling. Four months into parenting, and already the contrast between physical constraint and a churning mind had become characteristic of the venture for me, but I'd not yet felt it to this extent. I sat within a tent of love and agony and impatience, the small space filling with my hot breath, the arrhythmic pulse of our two hearts. And then he roused again. He arched his back and twisted his face and gave a bleating cry. He dove to my breast for comfort and rooted furiously. I felt the letdown, but he was beyond the help of milk. In fact, it made it worse. He pulled away. He was full-bellied and in pain. I elevated him and patted his back to soothe him, but it was no use.

There was acid in his belly. There was acid rising up our throats. It stings. It burns. Where do we turn for succor? Here? There? Nothing works. The sleeping house filled with screams.

T he first time I told anyone I had been sexually abused was in 1980, when I was twelve. I told Heather Moosier, while we were standing in a tight vestibule at the college in Western Pennsylvania where both our parents worked. Every Wednesday, Heather and I walked up the hill from our Gothic junior high school to campus, where I took violin lessons and she studied flute. After the half hour, we'd walk together to the administration building where both our mothers were secretaries. Our fathers were professors. This was enough to bond us in our small rust belt town, where professional jobs were rare, but we hadn't really known each other. Neither had our parents—or not well. But hers had used the faculty directory to find our phone number and call one night to discuss the possibility of Heather taking lessons on the same day as I did so that we could walk together.

I can still hear the ring of the phone, a portent harmonizing with the notes from the opening bars of *All Things Considered* and cutting through the steam rising from spaghetti just poured into a colander. The window above the sink looked out onto a rural route and some woods, shadowy in the twilight. I'd been roaming the woods since kindergarten, just about; I'd been allowed far afield in every direction for years. Previously, I'd walked to violin lessons alone, and my family thought it a little odd that Heather needed accompaniment, especially since she was a grade ahead of me. But being requested as a chaperone for an older girl puffed me up, gave the walk the weight and gravity of a milestone.

"Yeah, sure," I shrugged. The indifference was put on.

I HAD LONG FRIZZY HAIR, braces, and elbows wider than my biceps. I was part of, if not a clique, a boisterous group of girls just learning to use eyeliner and curling irons. Heather was taller than any of us, with a cap of feathered auburn hair and heavy breasts, and she was quieter. Instead of a group, she had one best friend, Carrie. But Heather and I got along. She immediately took me into her confidence, and I learned what she and Carrie had in common: they were both having sex with their boyfriends.

Each week, the two of us would leave school and stop at the corner gas station for a snack, and then we would begin our trudge to the college, Heather informing me in her lispy, whispery voice of the dramas and logistics involved in early adolescent fucking. There were trysts in the walk-in cellar, broken rubbers, passed joints. There was the acknowledgement of which couple had done it most: Raymond and Carrie. Carrie lived, like Raymond and Heather's beau, in the decaying heart of our town, where houses were closer and neighborhoods had sidewalks. Heather had to get dropped off at Carrie's on the weekends from her home in an outlying development and hope that Tommy would come by. They were all four in the cellar the time Carrie got Raymond riled up and then withheld the rubber once his pants were off, teasing him.

"Carrie, you give it here!" Heather mimicked his deep-voiced, tight-lipped delivery and then broke into a helium giggle that doubled her over.

I tried to join in but could not find the humor, could not even fake it. I was agog. Raymond was short but explosively muscular, with shoulders like a steel beam. His sprint times had attracted attention from the high school football coaches, and this, along with his unsmiling intensity and the fold of skin above his brow, gave him the air of a man. I'd never spoken to him. That slight little Carrie would tease him in the face of his anger, that she felt safe enough to, that she was so far from his urgency herself even as she flitted in her underwear in front of two boys moments away from letting one stick it in her . . . My synapses were firing like rockets. I might have looked like a scrawny child, but my interest was keen.

I'd been introduced to the pleasures of salacious reading material via the underlined V.C. Andrews novels passed through my sixth-grade classroom. I'd graduated in junior high to slipping books out of the public library—*The Mating Dance, The Joy of Sex, Love Machine*—and hiding them in my pillows to pore over at night. I felt lucky to have found a firsthand source of information in Heather, to peep in on real lives that matched the drama on the pages I was queasily drunk on. Carrie was performing the tease, just as Cathy Dollanganger had done to her mother's second husband in *Petals on the Wind*. Just like the big-breasted actress had done to the famous nightclub singer in *Valley of the Dolls*. But the plot arcs of the novels left no question about what these characters had wanted in exchange for the sex they advertised and then withheld. I wasn't sure of Carrie's aim. She had from Raymond all she could get from him; she'd given what she had. And there she stood dangling a rubber. Laughing in her underwear. In front of two boys. One with his dick out. The scene Heather had drawn hovered before me, more vivid than the sagging asbestos-sided homes that lined the sidewalk beneath our feet, but just out of reach.

As we walked on those afternoons, our instruments would bump against our knees, the oft-gray sky would darken further. Most weeks Heather could offer a new installment of her sex life. After Raymond broke the rubber two times, he started doubling up. One week Tommy decided that instead of letting her toke from the joint herself, Heather could only inhale what he delivered shotgun style. Listening, I would consciously savor the cream dollop in the center of my second Ding Dong. At home, sweets were counted out parsimoniously—five M&Ms at a time, one half of an off-brand pastry snack—and having a twin pack of Hostess to myself was decadent.

Heather, doing most of the talking, didn't have time to eat. She would begin to pant softly about halfway up the steep incline. She regularly voiced a worry that her parents would smell the cum on her.

"You can smell it?" I asked. "What's it smell like?"

"Oh yeah," she said. "It just does."

MY VIOLIN TEACHER was a man with a dramatic forelock and intense brown eyes who seemed to loathe accepting my check—we paid fifteen dollars for thirty minutes. It was three dollars more than the last instructor charged before he escaped to greener pastures, and my mother complained about the increase, hesitated each week with furrowed brow over her signature. I was working on the theme from Ravel's *Bolero* that winter, and the instructor and I were twinned in our humiliation: mine over having my parents pay someone to listen to me struggle with the notes; his, presumably, over the paltry price for which he sold his trained and refined ear to an unexceptional school girl. One day, he grabbed my violin from me and brought it alive, leaning into the mounting tune, filling the room with its demands.

"*That*," he said, swooping my revered instrument back to me as if it were nothing but a stick, "is how it should sound. *Feel* what you're playing."

I felt it. Oh, I felt it. I glared at him before tucking the violin back under my chin. I scraped the bow across the strings and fought back tears of shame and anger.

I HAD BEEN DRAWN TO MUSIC even before I had been drawn to whispers of masturbation, menstruation, and brassieres. There was the overheard, the glittery confetti of "Dancing Queen" at the ice rink, the slicked-up wail of Styx on a school bus eight-track. And there was my parents' record collection, folk and folk pop, and the corner nook between the couch and the love seat where the stereo lived and the albums were stacked and I could just fit, crouched or cross legged, flipping through the covers—the lady with whipped cream for a dress; Peter, Paul and Mary against a brick wall—while listening, listening. Airborne particles from the disintegrating cardboard sleeves singed like incense and made my nostrils burn. When in fifth grade a fiddle teacher had come to my school and played a tune, my chest creaked and billowed with the same majestic thwang as it did to the opening bars of my favorite Gordon Lightfoot song. I took up violin immediately, practiced assiduously, and made the all-city orchestra in short order.

But this passion of mine didn't last long. I had three teachers in four years, and something about the making of music was altered for me with that last one, squashed under his withering condescension, suffocated by the gendered gloomy sex vibe. Was the sex projected onto me or did I project it, clunking down the long music department hallway to his door each week with my hormones raging, my ears full of Heather's stories of dick and cum?

The question unfolds for me now: projected onto or projected by me? In its wake is the quiet as the needle pulls back from the record, lifts, retreats. Another album drops down. The skid of vinyl on vinyl. Judy Collins plays. Hers was among my favorites of my parents' LPs, and the song that most captured my imagination was her cover of "Suzanne." I loved it when the switch occurred, when finally *she* touched *his* perfect body with her mind.

I didn't share my parents' music with my friends. At school, it was Michael Jackson and AC/DC. I introduced Heather to the girls I knew. Her social circle expanded. Still, after many weeks of only listening, I felt like I had to contribute something to our conversations. Or maybe I felt I had to prove something, prove I was older than I looked, more mature than my behavior at my first make-out party suggested, where I'd opted to run races with the boys instead of neck in the woods with the one I'd been assigned. One evening, while Heather and I stood in the vestibule waiting for one of our mothers to drive us home, she was whispering on about penises and maybe I just grew tired of the dirty talk, of my nose being pressed to its glass, and I wanted to shut her up. Or maybe the dirty talk is what dredged up the memory, sunken in my mind, its features still muddy but suddenly recognizable. Suddenly nameable.

"The only hard penis I've ever seen is my cousin's, when he molested me," I said. "He used to come into my room at night when I was little."

Maybe I just wanted to see what would happen if I said it.

My eyes slid off Heather as I spoke. I looked out the safety glass of the vestibule door, which was crisscrossed with thin wire. Soft clumps of lamplit snow were falling from the black sky. There was a beat of silence. Then Heather asked in a low, solemn voice whether I'd told my parents.

I hadn't, and I flinched at the implication that I was a child, that I needed guidance and protection. Whatever I'd wanted to accomplish with my disclosure, it wasn't that. What did my parents have to do with anything? Had she told her parents that she whiled away her Saturday afternoons fucking? Had

Cathy Dollanganger told her mother that her brother had raped her (but only because he loved her so much)?

Of course, the difference was that I'd been so young. I'd said so explicitly. What I hadn't said was that in some ways the teenage encounters I was now reading and hearing about didn't seem all that different from what had happened to me. My sixteen-year-old cousin had started out wheedling and whispering, silently fumbling, asking awkward questions about what felt good—like any teenage boy might, in the basement with a girl. Then he abandoned persuasion and courtship on the day—I'd recently turned five— he finally took his penis out. Except for my very young age, that part of the story seemed common, too—an overpowering male, a female's will ignored. The memory of it was like breath under covers, too close. Heat was blasting from the vestibule's vent and inside my coat my armpits were sweating, but my feet were still cold. A gulf opened between Heather and me; while her confessions had brought us intimacy, now the boat on which I sat was moving farther from her shore.

It seemed to me then that the onset of womanhood—or more to the point, of sexy teenaged girlhood, of thrill—was all about externalization: boobs popping, menstrual blood flowing. None of this had happened to me yet, but something had. It had. It had. These other things were taking forever, but I'd been carrying this for so long, wondering what it was, waiting for it become clear. Now, finally, someone was talking about penises! Didn't offering one up make me a teenager? Perhaps not, said Heather's pause.

I stole a look at her. She resembled her mother—same auburn hair, full bust, round face, and ruddy cheeks—and never more so than now. She'd squared her jaw at my admission, her underbite becoming more pronounced above the ruffle of her plaid blouse. Her stern remove bit my skin. Shame oozed into my veins, something I'd only felt an inkling of before. It was creeping curiosity, mostly, or dumbfoundedness, that had previously slicked my memories of the bedside visits, when they arose at all. Still, I anticipated some sort of momentous alteration after sharing my news, believing I had been changed by the telling of a sex story, by using the word *molestation* in relation to myself.

BECAUSE IT'S A BIG DEAL, right? The happening of it? The naming it? Or is it not? For many years after that first telling I was unsure, confused by cultural messages and my own shifting responses, the different ways my memories could be made to fit with the identities I was trying to form. I don't recall telling anyone else about what my cousin did to me until I had moved out of our family home. It took me even longer to realize that Heather's instinct to connect my parents to what took place in my childhood bedroom was not entirely misplaced, however much I didn't want that to be true.

My cousin Toshi first came to live with us in the early 1970s, when he was sixteen. My father's brother had asked my parents to take him in after he and his second wife couldn't figure what else to do with him. Toshi'd been arrested. He'd run away from home. They couldn't keep him.

Toshi was the oldest of the five kids in the house, with one full sister, Haruna, and three much younger half siblings. In my head, I referred to the whole brood as "my Japanese cousins." My uncle had been born in Pittsburgh during the Depression to working class Jewish immigrants, but at eighteen he joined the military and was stationed as a member of the occupying army in Japan, and it was in that culture that he found his life's calling. On the GI Bill, he studied Asian literature, and not only did he become a translator and scholar of Japanese texts and a professor at a respected university, he also, in my view, and I imagine in his own, became Japanese. "He insists that the children only speak Japanese at home," clucked the grown-ups to each other, in tones alternating between admiration and skepticism. "Next fall they're going back to Tokyo again, but only for six months this time."

I was suitably mystified and impressed by these tidbits, in large part because he and the word "Japanese" correlated to the wedding portrait that figured prominently in the family photo gallery on the stairwell at my grandparents' house and in my imagination. In it, Morris and his Japanese bride are both wearing kimonos. His is plain and dark, bisected with a blindingly white sash, hers pale and elaborate, with a huge bustle. His hair was black, his eyes narrow triangles, his thick brows writ over them like calligraphic dashes on his dark complexion—nothing marked him as American. Her face was painted alabaster except for the rose bud of ruby staining the center of her lips. Her glossy hair was sculptural, spiked with combs and tasseled sticks— everything about her was Japanese.

I stood on the stairwell and stared and stared. At her, mostly. That a human being could look like that. That a visage so foreign had anything to do with me. The only thing competing for my attention in the small, plain house was a Japanese doll, maybe eighteen inches high, that lived in a glass display box on the buffet in the dining room, a gift from my uncle. Her face bore the same elegant, drawn-on expression my aunt's did. Her ebony hair was arranged with the same battalion of ivory and silk. The square sleeve of her brocade kimono dangled as she held out her arms just so, one hand displaying a fan shot through with silver, one thin white finger of the other kissing the thumb. She posed with a slight bend at her waist, an accommodating posture. I was doll crazy, and I desperately wanted to take her out of the box—I could see the small black hook where the door to the case was fastened. But I was never allowed.

I equated the doll with the bride in the picture. I equate the bride with Toshi's mother Chiyo, who Morris married in Japan and then brought back with him to New York City, where he was studying. But I could be wrong. Why would my grandparents keep portraits of the deposed wife? Perhaps, like me, they were captivated, proud to be associated with something so far away, so different.

"Were your parents upset when you married a goy?" someone asked my father once. I listened intently, always interested in lines of difference, in what it meant to be Jewish, in how adults explained themselves to each other.

"My brother had already married a Japanese woman," my dad said in a cocksure tone I didn't recognize. No one asked whether his parents were upset about that, but there was no sign that they resisted acceptance by the time I was studying for clues. Morris and Chiyo married in the 1950s when memories of World War II were fresh, when many Americans viewed the Japanese with suspicion and abhorrence. My grandparents had both been born in Eastern Europe, had lost relatives in Hitler's camps. Did they have some capacity for accepting difference that contributed to the intellectual curiosity and upward mobility of all three of their living children? As I struggle to get my own kids to try hard at anything, I've wondered at the past generation's secret. But if my grandparents were particularly open-minded, the doll and the portrait were the only evidence of it I noticed in their sunless lives.

MORRIS LEFT CHIYO. He ended the marriage when the children were young, and he claimed Toshi and Haruna entirely. There was the sense that he had snatched them. I asked my father how he could do this. I don't recall how old I was at the time, whether I was closer to being a child or an adult. My father's face clouded with concern when he answered. He chose his words carefully; they came with difficulty. Were there things he believed I couldn't understand, or didn't want me to have to?

What I remember of his response was this: "She couldn't speak English well. She was very vulnerable."

WHEN MORRIS REMARRIED, it was to the Japanese babysitter he had hired to look after Toshi and Haruna. She had cared for these children of the previous marriage for years, but living with Toshi became untenable to her. He had to go. If not to our house, then to some kind of institution.

IN PENNSYLVANIA, we told the story of the wicked stepmother. *She's mean to him*, were the whispers. We needed to explain how Toshi would cease to be a problem once he was ensconced in another home with young children. Otherwise, how could he be invited to live with us?

"She forces him to make everyone's beds."

"She yells at him all the time."

"She's mean to him now that she has her own."

FROM WHERE I STAND NOW, simultaneously a parent, daughter, sister, wife, a child, my heart goes out to everyone in this scenario. To my uncle, a disciplined man facing an uncontrollable adolescent and a frustrated second wife. To the wife, Yoshiko, birthing and caring for a string of babies in a house ruled by a controlling patriarch. I imagine the tide of prenatal and postpartum hormones rushing, the footsteps of the angry teenager rocking the floorboards, the heart thumping in martyred fury as the yelling wakes the baby again. And my heart goes out to my own mother, raising two very little children without much outside support in a home that must have already seemed cramped. And to my father, a deeply kind and generous man who likes to soothe all passages. He was being asked to give a home to his nephew or watch the boy go without, even though taking him would likely displease his already frustrated wife and disrupt his own fledgling family. A no-win situation.

And certainly my heart goes out to teenaged Toshi, banished from his home. Seen as a burden, the bearing of which had to be pleaded and compensated for. There are few takers for stray teenagers, those monsters of mood, oil, limbs, sex, and stink. What a time to be thrust out to stalk the earth. It's even more painful to consider the plight of young Toshi and his sister. For the two young children taken from their mother, gone. To not be mother-loved.

But my empathy flows most fully when it comes to the one person in the scenario about whom I know the least: Chiyo, a Japanese immigrant alone in the United States in the early 1960s. Stripped of her children. Abandoned. Beautiful. Foreign. Each of her weaknesses turned against her. In any game of moral relativity it's the children who demand our greatest sympathies. They're always entirely guiltless, absolutely vulnerable—at what age is this no longer true? But Chiyo's loss taps into some of my most anxious fears as a mother—that I will make the wrong decision, that my character will be found wanting, that some consequences are irrevocable, and the life-long well-being of my child is constantly on the line.

My heart goes out. To the mothers. To the fathers. To the children. To that mother. To that child. It's a complicated knot.

AND SO TOSHI CAME TO US, the threads entwining us, and we were knotted, too. But first came some cash. My uncle and aunt forked something over so we could make the necessary accommodations, and perhaps this money was as much of a factor in my parent's acceptance as was familial generosity, filial loyalty, and avuncular concern. Despite my dad's steady academic job and our modest lifestyle, finances were always tight. My parents hired workers to build a room in the basement, laid orange indoor-outdoor carpeting, and bought a dehumidifier. When Toshi came, my mom took him shopping and let him pick out his own sheets, wild ones that lived in our family for years—rain slicker yellow with a pattern of sketched-on black octagons. My mother disapproved of the choice. She disapproved of him almost immediately.

"He acts like the kids aren't even here," she told my father repeatedly.

I remember arranging army men on a playroom battlefield with a boy from the neighborhood when Toshi walked past in a whoosh, a wash of black hair, a big belt buckle.

"He acts like we're just not here," I parroted to my friend.

BUT I KNEW he knew I was there. I shared a small bedroom with my younger brother on one end of the narrow, slant-ceilinged second floor. My parents' room was at the other end of the hall. The enclosed staircase—separated from the first-floor hallway by a door—ran up the middle of the house and let out right in front of my threshold. Soon after he moved in, Toshi began slipping into my room and getting into bed with me at night, asking in a whisper if I wanted to play a game. "It's a secret game I play with Haruna. Don't tell your mom and dad." I had never met Haruna, but I'd seen pictures. She was a big girl. She was beautiful.

I've always been a poor sleeper. I find it difficult to fall asleep; when I do, the smallest thing can wake me up, and letting go of consciousness again is hard. My father complains of this, too, but if I play the game of clear-cut causality, I wonder if my fight with sleep stems from being awoken so often at four and five years old. A pattern revealed itself. Recognizing it was my first conscious acquaintance with my own intelligence.

I grew to expect Toshi's entry if my parents were out. He'd slip in shortly after my brother and I went to bed. If my parents were home, as they usually were, he might come or he might not, and if he did it'd be later, his increased furtiveness obvious to me even back then, the door cracking open just far enough for a body to fit through sideways, the almost inaudible click as he slowly released the knob. Most nights I waited to see what would happen, silent and vigilant, grimly pleased with my forecasting abilities if the door opened when I thought it might. But if he didn't visit soon enough, nervousness or anticipation would eventually give way to sleep, and then there'd be the almost physical pain of having it disturbed when he came in.

"Are you sleeping? Are you sleepy?" His hands would already be on or in my underwear. I wanted to push the intrusion away, but my limbs felt tied at my side, they wouldn't obey my groggy brain. "Are you sleeping?"

"Mmmph."

"Are you sleepy?"

"Yes." During these first months, his insistent questions and his dismissal of my affirmative answer felt as assaulting as the touching itself.

"Are you still sleeping?"

I'd reply yes, but it would be a lie. Toshi would know it.

"Do you want to play our game?" The crux of the game at this point was which I liked better: to have him stroke my vulva with his hand over my underpants or beneath. I always replied that I liked it better over my underpants. The alternative made me squirm, felt sharp and prickly, like the sting from unwiped pee.

"Are you sure?" he would say. "Let me try it again a different way. What feels better, like this? Or like this?" There were many variations that had to be assessed.

If he entered the room before I fell asleep, the game elicited a combination of curiosity and stoicism from me. What was it that was happening? I usually tried to say as little as possible, to keep my answers monosyllabic, to take in more than I gave out so that I could gain some understanding and perhaps an upper hand. I recall this feeling vividly.

But at least one time I caved: "What did Haruna like better?" I remember asking. Even then my spoken words sounded pathetic and plaintive to my ears, but I was looking for a guide, wanting to bring her back into the room to release some of the lonely intensity, to make it more like a real game, to illuminate the mystery.

If he came in during the dead of the night, I had no curiosity. The doggedness of his fingers against my heavy body could be almost intolerable. Better not to be dragged from slumber if I could help it. Better to fight sleep off.

The second person I remember telling that I had been molested was a man I took up with when I was twenty. It's possible that I told other friends before then, but if I did, it was the same version I told Heather, it was a story of sexual activity passed like a V.C. Andrews novel. With Carl, it was a little different.

We had met in West Philadelphia in 1988, where I had moved for the summer to stay with Reba, my best friend from high school, who'd been renting out the attic in a group house. The decrepit Victorian was filled with anarchist kids and counter culture types, and was a gathering place for neighborhood squatters and itinerant punk rockers, with one or two hippies living in the school bus parked out front. I was as titillated in the presence of these colorful ragamuffins as I had been at twelve hearing about sex from someone who'd had it. I'd been attracted to alternative cultures even before I knew there were such things—since Suzanne in her rags and feathers, since the Clash appeared on *Saturday Night Live* and raised every hair on my body while the girl at whose house I was sleeping guffawed and mocked. I'd picked my college based on a belief that punk and bohemian types congregated there, and I'd made my plans for the summer between sophomore and junior year on a similar basis.

I had only been sort of right about the college. When I arrived at Oberlin, I was surprised to see so many copies of *On the Road* by bedsides and on bookshelves; hitherto I had felt the book to be my own personal bible, handed down to me by my special father and unknown to anyone else my age. But it took me less than a semester to realize that my fellow students were more likely to have bought their crushed velvet and cracked leather at Agnes B. than at Salvation Army counters, and to have slept off their CBGB's hangovers in homes on the Upper West Side rather than in an Alphabet City tenement, as I presumed real punks did. These differences mattered.

Meanwhile, plenty of my new acquaintances were surprised to learn that not everyone paid for SAT prep classes, and they were confused by rural experiences that weren't covered by Outward Bound tuition or had at a summer home, amused by the low prices in the town diner that was still too expensive for me to visit more than once a week, despite my food service job. Some of the big-city transplants were less incredulous about rust belt realities than wearied by them. Used to being among the financial and cultural elite, they were outspoken in their annoyance at the high number of fellow students who had been the strangest people in their Midwestern hometowns. They missed New York and compared notes about hot spots.

I had a complicated relationship to these cool-club rich kids ("rich" to me meaning anyone who didn't receive financial aid). I wanted in, to some degree—I certainly didn't want to be pegged as an outsider—and so I studied their habits carefully. I filed away the derisive comments, and used them to sharpen my sense of myself for years. But I also used them to blur my own origins. At my twentieth college reunion, when an undergraduate acquaintance told me that he'd always thought I was one of those people who attended Saint Ann's, a private high school in Brooklyn that bequeathed to Oberlin many a sartorially impressive art major, I felt, to my chagrin, as if I had won some kind of lifetime achievement award. But the victory was hollow, because I never wanted to be a daughter of the privileged set, exactly, or even to be seen as one. Despite my awe at my sophisticated peers and what had been accessible to them, I also maintained my own streak of separateness and superiority. Money itself did not impress me, and in my view it could hamper the ability to accrue what did: the accretion of gritty experience and the recognition of unvarnished truths about what life was really like—probably tough, messy, twisted. Though my college friends might have been to Paris and hung out in Washington Square Park, they were low on street cred. Not only was I convinced that I had some, but I believed that I, more than many of them, was primed to get more.

PHILADELPHIA WAS ALL ABOUT street cred. Although some of the West Philly people had finished college, a greater number had slipped away from homes made tumultuous by drug or alcohol abuse, by enraged or disengaged or dogmatically Christian moms, or by lecherous stepdads. Most of them earned what money they did off the grid, making armor or low-budget gay porn, selling plasma, renting themselves out to medical studies, dumpster diving to reduce the need to buy things. A few of the girls worked as strippers or prostitutes, and just as I arrived more young women were taking up that beat, getting on the roster to dance at the Bounce Babe Lounge, a little dive in Center City that had a low barrier to entry. Newbies often worked the day shift, and in my first few weeks in Philly I adopted a routine that included making the rounds of restaurants accepting applications, stopping by the ice cream parlor where Reba was scooping cones for minimum wage, and then heading a few blocks north to have a drink at the Bounce Babe.

Reba's brand new girlfriend Catanine, a butch dyke even younger than I who carried a staff, was a regular at the ice cream parlor and the Bounce Babe, too, but she and I didn't hang. She never sat at either place, and never partook of the free scoops or beer; she stood at one end of the freezer case or by the wall close to the door at the club, hands resting together on her carved stick, keeping an eye out. There was a coolness between us: I was miffed that she'd horned in, and she'd made no conciliatory gesture. She and Reba had gotten together on my very first night in town, laser-beamed into each other's eyes so deep that they must have teleported up the three flights of stairs into Reba's bed; I sure didn't see them leave from the front porch where a group of us had been sitting.

The woman whose room in the house I'd be subletting was not leaving until the next day, and the only place I had to sleep was on a mattress tucked in the rafters of the attic where Reba lived. Hours after the lovers disappeared, realizing that Reba was not coming back to escort me, I made my way up there, literally crawling on the floor to find my bed in a pitch black garret alive with sex sounds: the click of mucous membranes, the bedspring groan of bodies shifting, the paired and labored breathing. I finally slept, and when I woke, they were at it again, or still. I watched them. One minute. Two minutes. Three minutes. I recognized that waking in this attic to this sight was the type of vérite I'd craved, and I chalked up a tally, but the inevitability of loneliness settled into me. I would have to face this new environment alone.

I made my way to the kitchen, where I sat on a bench that ran along one side of the long table with my book in front of me, but with my eyes swiveling everywhere else. There was so much to see. Flyers for protests and political meetings and punk shoes were tacked on a bulletin board and layered on the refrigerator. Surfaces were crowded with stacks of paperbacks, cassette tapes with handmade covers, jelly jars filled with spices, dirty dishes, and canisters of bulk grains and legumes. And there was so much to smell. The parlor of the house acted as a bike room and erstwhile repair shop, and the stink of grease and tires permeated the whole first floor, laid just beneath the sweetening bananas in the hand-thrown bowl on the table, last night's curry, this morning's coffee, and the aroma of a warmed stovetop that was crusted and buckled like asphalt. I'd been in punk pads before—in Pittsburgh, in Philly, in State College—but this house was far richer, steeped deep in every countercultural trend of the last thirty years until it smelled of them all.

And the people! A constant flow in and out, they emanated exotic oils and their own B.O., and they were beautiful to me. Hair dread-locked or Manic Panicked or shaved off, clothes ripped and rejiggered and worn with élan, and among the male residents were a few who were men to my eyes, so clearly different from the student boys with whom I'd been cavorting—towering over them, for one, was there something in the bananas?— that it was hard to believe they shared a Y chromosome. At Oberlin, a school then known for the lax hygiene of its crunchy granolas, I was still on the grungy side of average, but here, I felt squeaky clean, a square, a completely uninteresting summering college student who could not possibly register on anyone's radar.

On anyone's radar, that is, except those looking for a potential sex part-ner. Which, okay, was the status of a not insignificant number. So while "the real me" felt invisible, another me felt on display, on the shelf at a market. And, to be fair, I had put myself there. If my advocate at this house had aban-doned me, I was going to need another one, because, hey, this was where I wanted to be—absolutely, without a doubt. And while my belief that gaining the sexual interest of the right person was the shortest route to belonging might have been complicated by my declaration of a women's studies minor earlier that year, it had not been supplanted. Especially when my best friend was busy fucking someone else and the guys were this hot.

"I'm Reba's friend," I'd offer when acknowledged. "I'm going to be rent-ing Secil's room." I was alone, out on plank dangling over something new and unknown. I found I liked the feeling.

Which was good. Because did Reba and Catanine never have to pee? Did they never have to eat?

"I'm still waiting for Reba to come down," I said to one of the very tall men the second time he came through the kitchen and raised his heavy eye-brows at me.

"She's leaving you sitting here a long time." His eyes traveled down and up before locking on mine. I felt condescended to, and shamed, and seen. My nipples and clitoris buzzed.

"Yep."

"I'm going into Center City to check out a festival later. If she isn't down by then, you can come if you want."

Here we go here we go here we go, I thought. But I tried to act blasé.

CARL LOOKED LIKE a young Marlon Brando, stretched thinner but with shoulders as wide in his black leather jacket and a temperament as broody, and he was worldly wise at the ripe old age of twenty-four to my just-turned twenty, taller than I was by almost a foot. Public Enemy's *It Takes a Nation of Millions to Hold Us Back* had been released a couple months previous, and Chuck D's insistence and the steady squeal of "Don't Believe the Hype" unfurled from cars into the street that afternoon as it would the whole hot summer, rattling mufflers and internal organs before receding again from the ears of pedestrians, the thump-thump-thump the last to be heard, the lyrics still ringing in my head—"but some they never had it"—until another pair of chromed hubcaps would appear and externalize the track again. It was a long walk to the festival, which had something to do with Africa, or Black Pride, and when we got there the scent of sandalwood incense was heavy in the air.

When we'd exhausted what the fair had to offer us—spectacle, mostly, the feeling of being other together—we went to a bar where we drank round after round of Colt 45, which Carl paid for. I ran out of my Camel Lights and switched to his Reds. Somewhere along the way he dropped his cool and became chatty, explaining the mechanics of the house to me in all their gossipy glory. He laid out the tension between the more dedicated political anarchists and the anarchically libertine, told me the histories of recent residents and their replacements, detailed whose yearnings for whom had been kindled, returned, rebuffed in storylines involving twists of sexual orientation and both principled and not-quite-so non-monogamy. I raked it all in as if I were studying for a high-stakes final while I gulped my beer and batted my eyes at him.

"Are you an anarchist?" he asked me.

"I don't know," I said. Anarchism wasn't en vogue at Oberlin. I could tell that the house members who were part of Wooden Shoe bookstore collective didn't have too much to do with the circled A of the Sex Pistols, but that was about it. "Are you?"

He paused thoughtfully. "I'm a Situationist."

"What's that?"

"You never read Guy Debord at that fancy college?" We'd already established that he knew about Oberlin. A woman on the scene, an elegant junkie from money who'd never stopped slumming, had gone there, too, for a while.

"No."

"I'll loan it to you. After you read it, then we'll talk. Are you a feminist?"

"Yes."

He gave a rueful grin. I congratulated myself on the right answer, true and sexy.

IT'S AMAZING HOW FAST identities shift and gel at that tender age. Six months earlier, Reba had been renting a room from a yuppie graphic designer in Center City. I had come to visit over winter term to intern at the feminist paper, and we'd tiptoed around the city she was still finding her way in, trying to slip into cool clubs or bars, then standing at the edges of them. It'd only been a year since I'd simultaneously discovered vibrators and Kathy Acker, two things that seemed absolutely essential to my notion of myself as I sat twisting next to Carl on the barstool that day.

Reba had sent the vibrator to me in New Mexico, where I was spending the summer. It was a huge, Caucasian penis model powered by D batteries that she'd picked up at a corner porno store. Acker's novel *Don Quixote* I had special ordered at a Santa Fe bookshop, a waitressing job finally providing me with the money to pay for it after I'd been carrying around a review of it for months. I expected the book to be a revelation, and it was. Reading it, I felt discovery and recognition even when I couldn't understand what Acker was saying. Unfamiliar with the original *Don Quixote*, I couldn't use it as a template, but Acker's protagonist was made a knight by receiving an abortion, I understood that much. I sensed some truth about armor and pure resolve arising from violence and shame, and the way this inevitably led to sexing with multitudes, with people of every age and gender variation and also dogs. *YES!* I wrote in the margin. The book's exuberance and lack of plot stimulated and exhausted me and often sent me back to bed, where I'd probably just come from anyway, since I spent a lot of time there with the vibrator. Sometimes I combined activities, and used the vibrator while reading. Each orgasm grew up from my toes.

I TROTTED OUT Acker's name now, the coolest one I knew. Carl hadn't read her, but he knew of her, he approved. He'd heard she was a Burroughs disciple.

"No she wasn't! That's not true!" I cried out. I had no idea, really, but I couldn't allow the fierce knight Kathy Acker to be slotted as the little sister of the guy who'd shot his wife in the head. Burroughs's punk godfather status and his renowned act of misogyny created the kind of uncomfortable dissonance in my head that make me argue with any boy listening. But at that point in the day, in the drinking, in the opening bars of our relationship, my stridency floated right past Carl.

"Have you ever been in love, Zoe?" His chin was on his fist, his eyelids at half-mast, his eyes on mine but slightly unfocused.

"Yes," I said, relieved that my sword wasn't needed to defend Kathy Acker's honor and that I could slip back into being a courted girl who prided herself on using honesty as a method of flirtation. "I have." I gave a heavy sigh as if love's ravages wearied me, and then I looked up from my beer with a knowing smirk.

I'd met my guitar-playing boyfriend my freshmen year, and he'd been my first real lover, the first person with whom I both figuratively and literally slept on any kind of regular basis. It wasn't long before we were practically symbiotic, informing each other's speech patterns and thesis sentences and food choices, growing what appears now in the few photos that exist to be a single mop of unruly hair and engaging in passionate deconstruction of our every utterance, especially on the subjects of power, gender, genius, sex. Although we'd had a rocky road the last couple months of school, under the pressure of his graduating and the future's uncertainty, he was coming to Philadelphia in a couple weeks to live for the summer because I was there, a fact that was dissolving in my mind like a sugar cube dropped into beer. I let my answer stand unelaborated upon, an implied past tense. Walking back to West Philly in a haze of Colt 45 and chemistry, I was already gone. I had gnawed off that important relationship and left it behind in the bar as if it were a limb in the maws of a trap.

CARL AND I didn't sleep together that night or the next night. I don't remember how many days later it was that I made my way to his room. I don't remember his invitation, or how I got there, or if I had officially broken up with my boyfriend yet or not. But I can almost smell the chemical firing from my brain being blown. He lived on the third floor in what had once been a kitchen. Against one wall remained a sink and some cheap cabinets, and against another a few plastic milk crates held albums. A mannequin wearing a gas mask stood guard in one corner. There was no other furniture. We sat on opposite sides of the mattress on the floor for a brief, loaded exchange of sentences, and then he crawled toward me slowly, his large face coming first, pointy-chinned like a cat, thick lips protruding. It was the last moment of calm.

He was less like Marlon Brando in bed and more like the Transexual Transvestite from Transylvania. He was hypermasculine and campily feminine. He was huge and graceful and sure and louche. He had swiveling hips and a massive finger span and no shame. He was not afraid of any part of me and not afraid of hurting me or displeasing me. He was greedy, but also baldly fascinated by my avidity and receptivity. The strokes of his dick unloosed in me every pornographic cliché I'd imbibed in my near decade-long exploration of smut prose: *I'm impaled*, I thought ecstatically. *He's in me up to my throat!* As each worn phrase exploded through my consciousness I felt like I was meeting truth, being made real. When he came I clutched at what I thought was the end before discovering his first orgasm was like my own, less a satisfaction than an antagonism, just a vista on the way to the top of the mountain—grandeur, yes, ahhhh, have a drink—but then back to got-to-get-there, got-to-get there, higher, more. It was a sweltering night and the sheet soon pulled off and the texture of the worn mattress was pilly and disgusting. Our fingernails filled with the black of each other's dead skin. Sweat slicked our bodies. Even hours into it, his penis thwacked back toward his stomach when I let it go. His moves had been impressive, but then we went to a place beyond moves. We were not so much communing as erupting.

At one point, we lay apart, backs propped against the wall, legs splayed, touching just at our hooked ankles, both twitching, in a fevered trance. I was brought back to myself by the arrhythmic shaking of the mattress; I saw he was jerking himself off, the streetlight coming in and laying blue on our bodies. I watched him. *So this is what we were going to do now*, I thought. I touched myself too, but my fingers didn't feel good in the raw folds, and he was oblivious to me. Without his interest I became confused. I took a breath and rolled toward him, straddled high on his thigh and moved my mouth towards his head.

"I don't know what you want me to do," I whispered. Our skin was sticky, and it hurt as it pulled at each shift of weight. "Tell me what you want me to do." I had never said this to anyone before.

Carl returned back to the room. He smiled at me with surprise, a conde-
scending kindness. He didn't tell me anything, but he kissed me deeply. He
put his hands on my hip bones and pressed while he set me back, which made
me feel tiny and invincible. My blood rose again.

We had sex until my body was battered. Until my pussy was so swollen
the only thing to make it feel better was to get it wet all over again, until a single finger in me felt as huge as a giant cock, until uncertainty was obliterated.
He staggered off to work the next morning after a single hour of sleep. After
a few more, I wobbled down to see Reba at work.

"I thought you two might get together," she said to me calmly, perhaps
even coolly. She coaxed a ball of ice cream from the vat and then glided down
the counter to give the customer their cone and take their money.

There might have been a recent history of perceived betrayals that each
of us was retaliating against that summer, the confused pain of separation
that is part of youth and love and growth. Was she leaving me behind as she
became more big-city punk rock? Was I snubbing her in favor of snooty college intellectuals? Maybe a little of both. We were both horny girls who had a
fierce attachment that we'd never explored physically. Between Reba's sexual
enlightenment and my own and our need to differentiate, the main times she
and I talked privately during that fervid June and July were the few occasions
when she got off work early and, having an hour to kill before Cantanine
came to get her, accompanied me to the Bounce Babe Lounge.

T here was no cover, no doorman. No one batted an eye when we walked in, underage and in ratty clothes cadged from laundry left too long in communal dryers. Most days, I sat alone at the far end of the bar, watched the girls dance on the tiny stage behind it. There were just a few on shift at a time. I had started coming at the invitation of Maerene, a young Irish expat who squatted in West Philly and hung out on the porch of the anarcho house. She wore wigs over her shaved head, bobby socks with her stilettos, and a kimono in between sets. She was gently pear-shaped, and her long limbs had little discernable muscle tone—the exact opposite of the other woman I recall easily, a petite heroin addict from outside the an-archo-punk clan who had breasts like pesticide-plumped red apples and the taut musculature of a gymnast wrapped in waxy, bruised skin. She was fine-featured and wore her hair in a tight ponytail. Her boyfriend famously let her dance as long as she kept her bra on, but some afternoons she'd show up desperate, begging to be let on the shift, and she'd strip down to pasties for the bigger tips while nervously keeping an eye on the door. The girls chose songs from the jukebox when it was their turn on the stage—mostly

Top 40, hard rock, and funk. They danced each in her own style, and they were good. I liked to watch them.

I watched the way Maerene and the other new girls, all of whom were my new housemates and neighbors, adopted the stripper moves and then made them their own, the Americans adding touches whose provenance I recognized from childhood dance classes and MTV music videos. I watched the heroin addict execute pro stripper moves like a machine, kicking up the pole into an upside-down straddle, bending at the waist, ass towards audience, jiggling her butt cheeks so they slapped together rhythmically (I was astounded that such firm butt cheeks could do that). She rotated vigorously through half a dozen of these operations with no worry about adding flow in between them. On the other side was loungey Maerene, who was nothing but flow. I watched her strut on the eight-foot-long platform and twirl languorously, letting a gauzy scarf slip off her shoulders, slinking her arms free of her bra straps so that the soft cups flapped below her budded breasts like an unhooked garter belt. She never broke a sweat.

Neither did I, surprisingly enough for a young women's studies minor who just a month or two earlier had penned a writ-in-blood paper about the pernicious effect of sexed-up photos of women in *Rolling Stone*, and who had lacerated her boyfriend for the small collection of ass shots he'd clipped from old copies of *Penthouse*. I boiled with feminist rage that year; it pounded in my blood like fists against a wall. When my boyfriend sat on my dorm room bed with his guitar and sang an angry song he had written about me—or was it about another girl? It hardly mattered; my reaction was the same when it was my turn—my vision of kicking the instrument to smithereens was so intense I blinked when he finished, as if emerging from a darkened theater, surprised to find I had not moved from my cross-legged seat on the floor. I wanted and hated having a song written about me. I wanted and hated how transported he was while he played it. I loved and resented how intensely certain live music made me feel, and how that intensity of feeling wasn't translatable in the boy-rock world, where factual knowledge and expertise were the currency. These passionate contradictions combined with my sexual shame—for my hunger, for my clumsiness, for my secrets—and with the salt of the disregard and violations I perceived as having been inflicted upon me due to my gender. All this I was pouring into a new pot, splattering as I did so, where it stewed in the context of histories I was learning about, of cosmologies and systems. I was trying desperately to sort out the feelings and the theories, to read enough and think enough and write enough to name them, but that's hard to do at a full boil. My sophomore year in college was wonderful and important for me, but I was pretty much the opposite of chill.

Yet there in the neighborhood strip club, I found some relief. My efforts to suppress the nervous mix of arousal and misgiving I felt when pushing open the heavy black door were so easily successful as to be eager. The permission I gave myself to be there (and received from the indifferent establishment and the West Philly milieu), along with the beers I drank and the chain of Camel Lights I smoked and the aftershock endorphins from the prior night's long fucking, sedated me into a narcotic repose after my couple years of tension. In the presence of so many available women, the occasional man who sidled up to me never pressed the issue when I demurred attention. Hey, I was just there to see my friends. I was just another lazy afternoon patron, if with a funny little twist—escaping from my job search and internal unrest, letting myself be soothed by watching pretty, nearly-naked women dancing.

THE WOMEN ALL told me the vibe was different at night. Even in daylight, their enchanting performances on stage didn't yield the dancers any tips, and I wasn't so sedated that I didn't notice how they had to labor and grind for those, hop down, work the bar, make eye contact while shimmying their tits and brazenly pressing for money. The calculated exchange, callous and begrudged on both sides, that was the part I felt embarrassed to be seeing, but I looked hard at it, even if through lizard eyes. The lizard eyes of a stoned anthropologist. I collected raw material for my sense-making project and for catching my buzz. In between their sets and tips-rounds, I'd chat with my housemates. It made me feel special, because they'd talk to me for free.

It seemed that every day another West Philly girl was taking up dancing. Many of them encouraged me to give it a shot. They were sure I'd be hired. The owner of the Bounce Babe liked skinny white girls with long dark hair, they said. They were confident in the knowledge of his preference, which he'd offered in a tutorial about how every man had them and how to divine those of clients without taking it personally. But despite fitting his bill, I didn't jump. Why not, they wanted to know—it had become almost de rigueur among the unemployed in the house, and they all knew I was looking for a job.

"You're there all the time anyway," Maerene pointed out to me.

"I'm not the stripper type," I said. I pointed at my chest. "Tiny boobs."

"I've seen your nipples!" she cried. She was well into her forty-ouncer and who knows what else. "You can do it. They're cute!"

They were probably flashing as she spoke, because another girl was behind me giving me a shoulder massage and my tank top had loose armholes and I seldom wore a bra. I was not ashamed of my small breasts. I liked them fine; I liked the freedom they gave me, and it seemed almost incidental to me to cover up. But although when my Oberlin boyfriend came to town I wouldn't even let him climb the stairs of the porch when he walked me home, so afraid was I of being seen as a sheltered college girl, I maintained my resistance to stripping even at the risk of appearing prissy, of not fitting in. I didn't want my breasts to be rated by the same men I peacefully sat alongside at the strip club. I knew my comfort in my body would be mitigated by the judgment, and that the defenses I'd need to build up against it, and against monetized interest and stolen gropes, would alienate me from my newfound ability to see sexual energy as a fuel for anarchic revolution rather than a ball in the Bobby Riggs-Billie Jean King tennis match. Even at ten dollars an hour plus tips and street cred, it wasn't worth it.

I take my son and daughter to my friend's place to celebrate her forty-fifth birthday. Connie's been separated from her husband for almost a year, and her life has settled into a new groove—new apartment, new friends, new man in her life. She's been dating this guy for a while, but I've yet to meet him, I've only heard tell. I'm looking to collect some first-hand observations before I wholeheartedly give my approval.

He's not there yet when we arrive, and we all settle into the living room—my daughter coloring with another little girl, my son playing video games with Connie's son, me bantering with the grown-ups, three sharp, divorced moms, about men, and sex, and male strippers. I tell them the story of how I waitressed at a Chippendales-type show at the Italian Civic Club when I was in tenth grade. We laugh and riff off each other, mix confession with salt and humor, speak either *sotto voce* or in a code we believe can't be read by the children—Chippendales, there's no way they know what that is, even if the tone of our laughter draws an antennae away from the glow of the high definition screen. I'm conscious of how fresh the conversation seems in comparison to those I have with married women in my neighborhood and at school functions. I'm aware of how familiar and foreign it is, a diet I used to live on and seldom taste now. I want more. I don't really want my friend's new boyfriend to show up with his two sons and break the all-girl vibe.

But then Connie's son starts asking her every few minutes: "Why aren't they here? When are they coming? Shouldn't they be here by now?" His anxiety gives voice to the rest of ours. He should be, shouldn't he?

"Quit asking," Connie finally snaps. "I don't know where he is. He's not answering his phone." I feel the moms circling the wagons around our friend, some of us turning toward her, ready to offer any comfort, some of us facing outward, cocking our guns for an attack. Why *aren't* you here, motherfucker? My desire to vet this guy goes from passive to active, the benefit of my doubt no longer assured.

But then the doorbell rings and the new gang troops in merrily, the boyfriend with his two growing sons, and he handles the situation so comfortably. Within a few sentences, I'm ready to like him. We share some room on the couch. Another of the moms and the man volley about the first date she's going on later, what signals her clothing sends. The evening is just getting started, and I'm relieved to see it's going to stay slightly ribald and fun.

It's an Indian summer night, mid-October, deliciously warm. My daughter had insisted on wearing her new Halloween costume to the party, a furry bear suit, and I had said she could as long as she put on shorts underneath rather than the pants she'd been wearing, so that she wouldn't get too hot. She gets too hot despite my forethought, and within an hour she wiggles out of the costume, the pelt of russet fluff and cheap sateen discarded on the floor. She vaults onto my lap. She's a climby girl, squirmy, long-legged, and she twists from me to scale the back of the couch. She gets stuck for a moment with her head pointing to the ground and her little bottom lifted into the air, barely covered by the striped shorts that fit at the beginning of summer. My husband and I have oft remarked that one of the many details of parenthood that doesn't get relayed clearly is how consistently one's face will be put in close quarters with toddlers' butts and genitals. Almost daily, at times both expected and not, you'll be offered a full view of a winking asshole, a sticky scrotum, a stinky vulva. But at three and a half, in positions like the one she's in, my daughter's body is already becoming more like a girl's, less like a genderless toddler's. Next to me, the man says something like: "Whoa, I don't want to get arrested."

I know this can be a concern of men, a real one. My husband stayed home with the kids more than I did, and he'd mention times when he felt unwelcome on the playground because of his gender, get a dirty look from a mom if he tried to help a little one up the stairs of the slide. Another male friend talked about the awkwardness he'd felt when the little girl he'd been babysitting insisted he wipe her after she peed. Another friend had the police show up at his door because he had taken his daughter on a weekday afternoon into Walgreens to pick up the pictures that included some of her in the bathtub. I have sympathy for the fact that presumed sexual guilt is something men have to walk around with, something that complicates their taking on more public care-taking roles. Still, the comment from the boyfriend half-raised my hackles. Aren't we all supposed to pretend we don't see it when a kid's butt suggests something about sexuality for a split second? Aren't we supposed to swallow any discomfort if we can't simply turn away? But these questions last no longer than a pulse.

As we are preparing to leave, my daughter puts back on her bear costume and admires it in the full-length mirror by the door. How fun to be a stuffed animal! The rounded ears, the extra soft padded oval of tummy, the stubby tail, which she points toward the mirror and then cranes around to see. "Shake your tail," calls out the boyfriend from the couch. And perhaps any question formed never entirely dissolves. A mama bear rises up in me immediately, rears on hind legs, towering, teeth bared, claws slashing, roaring: *I'll rip your mouth off!* In his comment, I see my daughter stripped bare, her body placed on the stage of femaleness, in front of the judging eyes. *I will plow bloody rifts in those faces! I will scratch out those eyes!* I see the multitude who will be watching her—my fear informed by my own awareness of how I'd found myself gazing at my ten-year-old son's female friends—to see when they go into bud, how they swan out, to admire and imagine what they'll look like later. Is it the self-implication that chains my mama bear's ankle? The awareness that our sexuality is complex?

The cooing over my daughter's costume extended to the ladies' chorus: "Look at you!" and "Shake it!"

A couple of these women have known and adored my child since she was born. She's always liked their kind attentions. She likes to dance. "Booty dance," she'll say sometimes, and she'll push her butt out behind her and shake it. She likes the way it feels, I imagine, that basic human pleasure, exaggerating movements to match a beat. It's clear that she also likes the attention doing it gets her.

"This was so much fun," I say cheerfully, gathering up shoes, the mama bear still raging behind my skull, against my skin, but kept there while the cub wanders a wider circle. I want my daughter to have a fully developed sexuality, to be able to explore and play with sexuality. I want to remove shame from this process, and for her to escape the pressures of commodification and expectation. I want her to be free to find what gives her bodily pleasure. I have always wanted that for myself. I believe I've fought for that for myself.

But I feel in a flash a new sense, if not understanding, of the origins of the burka, the hijab, dress codes. *Cover up, please.*

The mama bear, claws slashing—how far is my reach? *All the rest of you, shut up, avert your gaze, keep your hands to yourself.*

"Thanks so much," I say. "Happy birthday. Nice to meet you. We'll see you soon."

The female body, even at the age of three, the site of so much.

TWO MEMORIES I HAVE.

One, being with my brother at a rest stop and playing in the pebbles of the parking lot. We were streaming the pebbles from our hands, making mountains, creating a crashing sound. A little girl watched us closely. She tentatively picked up a small handful of pebbles, let them drip from her palm. Instantly, her mom yanked her up, slapped her hand, wiped it, yelled, "You'll get filthy!" I remember feeling gratitude that I was not her, that my mom was letting us play. We played hard. We ran far. Prissy instincts were not indulged.

Then, when I was in first grade, I remember sitting cross-legged on the floor in the cafeteria. I had red tights on—red was my favorite color—and the seam of the crotch was visible. Another girl looked at me blankly.

"Ladies don't sit like that," she intoned. "Ladies keep their legs together. That's what my mom told me."

And I was grateful again not to have such a mother. And I don't want to be a mother like that. And I don't want anyone, ever, telling my daughter to shake her tail. Even if she likes it.

M ore to the immediate point of why I resisted employment at the Bounce Babe Lounge: I feared that performing sexuality for men would alienate me from my ecstatic and revelatory lust for Carl. And despite the power of this lust, we had enough obstacles. I'd broken up with my college boyfriend soon after he'd come to town, but that house in West Philadelphia was a confusing atmosphere in which to start a heterosexual romance, even if you weren't two-timing.

The trend toward sex work had fostered a male-female rift in the neighborhood, as the women took to equating men and johns and a couple of them dumped guys they'd been hanging out with. As fresh meat on the scene, my scent attracted both the girls newly interested in their own and the boys and men left hanging by the change-over. With little to do besides sit on the porch and take in the milieu, I accepted compliments and massages from anyone who offered, in keeping with the anything-goes atmosphere. It wouldn't have been cool for him to voice a complaint, but when Carl came home from work to find me receiving rubs on both my neck and my feet, or lifting up my arm so someone could examine the small tattoo I had near my armpit, he might ignore me for hours. Meanwhile, he was still hung up on a former house resident, and when she came around, he'd turn his his beam on her. We didn't act much like an overt couple around the pack in any case. We went on a group road trip where we didn't sleep in the same tent on the first night. We dropped acid together and then he went off to an over-twenty-one joint where I couldn't follow.

But at some point most every night he'd give me a signal and we'd go up to his room and enter our sex zone. And often enough, we'd sneak off the premises and prowl the city as a pair. We had things in common aside from our desire to abrade our bodies against each other's. A secret hankering for greasy pizza and fountain Cokes to relieve the house diet of vegan stir-fry, for one thing. A preference for the kind of dirty guitar rock just starting to be put out by Sub Pop Records over the thrashier, hardcore stuff of Alternative Tentacles, for another, along with a belief in the totemic power of record label names. And we both came from small town upbringings that left us with a bit of gee-whiz when our guards dropped.

Mostly what we had in common was a desire to explore the metropolis by foot. We liked to walk, and we crisscrossed the city—from the dilapidated industrial sites on the West Side, to posh Rittenhouse Square in Center City, to the Historic District farther east. We were all the way down at Penn's Landing the night he brought up the road trip that'd been in the air: He and three other guys had been plotting to pile in Mel's truck and head to San Francisco to visit Joe, a popular housemate who'd made the move west a few months back. The departure date had been set for two weeks out. But if I wanted to, he told me, he'd ditch the ride, and he and I could take the thousand bucks he'd saved from his job as a laborer and we could hitchhike there together. We wouldn't rush madcap; we'd stop for adventures. We'd crash with friends of friends. We'd go camping. He'd always wanted to hike in the Rockies. He'd spent some seasons backpacking in the Adirondacks, and he had all the gear.

We'd go on the road, is what I heard. *On the Road On the Road On the Road.*

"Yes!" I said. Of course I said yes. As soon as the words were out of his mouth I believed I'd orchestrated my entire summer, my entire romantic history, my entire life, exactly for this. Over the next couple of days, as we proved our sincere intentions—Carl told the other guys he wasn't going with them, and I told Reba and my parents our plan—we couldn't stop grinning at each other like a couple of excited kids.

THIS PERFECT ACCORD didn't last long. Before we even left, we reverted back to being guarded and sly when we were out of bed, suspicious of each other's motives. Perhaps this was justifiable, given the dynamics. I was beholden to Carl in many aspects. He was older, bigger, male, more established amongst the crowd we ran in. He carried the cash, the know-how, the sexual prowess; I needed these things from him, and I didn't like feeling needy. It made me defensive. He also had moods that dwarfed my own, and he was not above using both his strengths and his weaknesses as a way to draw me in, bind me tighter. He wanted a dedicated mate, one without an expiration date, and although I was besotted with him, even subservient to him in ways, we were both aware that in all our adventures, he was not only my leader/ lover but also my temporary prop. I had dreamed of traveling the country, and I knew how impossible it would be to do on my own. I was checking something off a list, and the next item on it would send me to England alone for a year abroad. Carl, however addictive the orgasms, however aesthetic his skills and his sorrows, was my love object but also the means for an American adventure that had to be completed by a deadline.

I had read, by this time, not only *On the Road* but also *Minor Characters*, by Joyce Johnson, who'd been Jack Kerouac's girlfriend during the period when his fame peaked. My dad's editor had sent me the memoir when he told her how entranced I was by the Beats, and I devoured it. I related to Joyce Johnson mightily, a bookish, middle-class girl called early toward the margins of culture. Starting at the age of thirteen, in 1949, she slipped out of her bourgeois apartment to go down to Greenwich Village in search of Real Life.

"Real life was sexual," she wrote. "Or rather, it often seemed to take the form of sex. This was the area of ultimate adventure, where you could dare or not dare."

I admired her. I recognized how much bravery it'd taken to move out of her parent's house and live alone as a single young woman at a time when few others did. How fashionably prescient she'd been to seek out opaque black tights from a dancer's supply store when garters, nylons, and white gloves were de rigueur.

I also felt aggrieved on Johnson's behalf and on behalf of all those with whom I shared a gender. The shame she had to undergo during her risky abortion. The mockery she endured as an ambitious female dreamer. I understood—as likely was my dad's editor's intent—that there were reasons beyond the individual why a woman hadn't written a Beat ode as similarly exuberant as *On the Road.* Johnson recounts how an English professor at the all-girls college Barnard introduced a course by asking how many of the students wanted to be authors. The class was required of creative writing majors, and, confused by a question whose answer was self-evident, all the young women slowly raised their hands.

The professor said he was sorry to see this. "First of all, if you were going to be writers, you wouldn't be enrolled in this class. You couldn't even be enrolled in school. You'd be hopping freight trains, riding through America."

The thoughts of eighteen-year-old Sylvia Plath would seem to corroborate this writerly inclination. In a journal entry from 1951 she tells of her "consuming desire to mingle with road crews, sailors, and soldiers, barroom regulars—to be part of a scene, anonymous, listening, recording . . . to sleep in an open field, to travel West, to walk freely at night." But she can't. "I am a girl, a female, always in danger of assault."

"Received wisdom of 1953," wrote Johnson of her professor's remark. Received wisdom, too, of decades before and after. I'd been inoculated with it. The worldview of *On the Road*, not *Minor Characters*, remained one of my deepest inspirations even as I studied up on the unique challenges and strengths of women. Mixed with my gratitude toward the editor who'd given me Johnson's book was a tinge of resentment. Had she thought to take my fantasy away from me? It wasn't going to work. A tip of my hat to Joyce Johnson, but I was going to do her one better. In her years with Jack, she had never traveled with him. He'd held out promises—meet me here, meet me there—but they always fell through. She never made it on the road. Sylvia never made it, either. But I was headed out in the rough, real world. And if I needed a man in my tool belt as a rape-prevention device, well, I'd found one for whom I also had a ravenous attraction. Didn't that disprove any accusation that I was either taking advantage of him or caving into gendered norms? I thought what I had with Carl was among the best kinds of male-female partnerships that could be achieved in an unequal world.

My attitudes about rape were based both on my personal experience with sexual assault and on the common assumption that when it came to sex crimes, the word *victim* was just about synonymous with the word *girl* or *woman*. As girls, the risk of sexual violence and violation was given as the reason for so many of the rules we were supposed to follow—how we should dress and act, where we should go and how we should get there, what kinds of jobs and places and people we should avoid and allow ourselves to be protected from. The risk of becoming a victim was one of the defining features that separated our gender from the other, a big part of what made us *girls* and them *boys*. In fact, so pervasive was this view that until 2012, many law enforcement agencies, including the FBI, defined for data purposes "forcible rape" as "the carnal knowledge of a female forcibly and against her will." There was no way, by some official measures, that men could even be considered rape victims.

But although girls and women are more likely to be victims of sex crimes than boys and men are (and trans people have the highest rates of victimizations) no one is safe because of their gender. Men are of much higher risk than common knowledge supposes.

According to the CDC's Adverse Childhood Experiences Study, the largest one of its kind, one in six men have experienced abusive sexual experiences before age eighteen.

According to Bureau of Justice statistics, about nine percent of all victims of rape and sexual assault over the age of twelve are male. It's likely these numbers are very low. For one thing, they were gathered from patients getting physical examinations through an HMO and from household surveys, respectively. Thus they exclude inmates, who are vulnerable to sexual assault while incarcerated, and who are reportedly more likely to have suffered physical and sexual childhood abuse in their past than those in the general population.

In addition, research shows that men and boys may also be less likely than girls and women to recognize themselves as having been sexually abused or assaulted in the first place—reflecting our cultural and in some cases, legal, resistance to seeing males as victims. In one study, fewer than a fifth of men with documented histories of sexual abuse identified themselves as having been abused. In contrast, almost two-thirds of women with similar histories identify themselves that way. Needless to say, people who don't identify themselves as victims are less likely to get help to understand and ameliorate the consequences.

Even men who acknowledge to themselves that they've experienced sexual violence might be reluctant to speak of it to anyone. Our culture assumes male sexual insatiability and sees the ability to protect oneself as a core element of manhood—making men even more likely than women, who also experience reservations about disclosing, to be ashamed by victimhood, or to be fearful they won't be believed.

In 2014, the National Crime Victimization Survey found that as many as thirty-eight percent of incidents of sexual violence were committed against men. In just under half of these incidents, a woman was the violator.

The impulse many of us have to refuse to let our daughter do something we'd let a son do is not as rational as it may appear. Girls and women are more vulnerable, but not *that* much more vulnerable. What does it do to our conceptions of ourselves if we absorb that knowledge, and act on it?

In preschool, my best friend was a boy. We devised elaborate SM-themed fantasies involving our teachers, especially the prettiest one—already, I'd intuited that the prettiest one is whom the story will happen to. In our imaginings, we imprisoned, humiliated, and tortured this teacher in every way we could conceive of. Sometimes she played along, sitting on a child-sized chair and pretending to cry while we piled the cardboard bricks around her. We invented this game around the time my own abuse began, during my last year of preschool before kindergarten, but I can't be sure exactly which game came first—the one Toshi devised or the one I did.

T oshi ran away from our house before he completed high school. Once he left, he never touched me again, but he maintained a role in our family. Upon his capture (if that's the right word), he stayed at a home for wayward youth on the edge of town until he turned legal age. Then, my dad arranged for Toshi to attend the college where he taught, tuition free, and to live in the dorms. A couple years later, without having graduated, Toshi joined the Army. But even after enlisting, he wasn't gone for good. When he served in the Philippines, we were sent pictures. When he was stationed in the States, he visited. When he was done with his service, he came back to the college to finish his degree. We were his main family, after all. Or we sort of were.

An older student by the time he returned to re-enroll, Toshi lived in an apartment near campus, but he brought his girlfriend to our house for dinner regularly. She was an artist who'd defected from mainland China, a striking and interesting person. I remember her sitting in the visitor's spot at our dining room table, her back to the bay window so that from my position across from her she was silhouetted by the black night.

We were glad to have her; she was easier to converse with than Toshi. One evening after the meal, she moved beyond small talk when conversation turned to life in China. Her voice became fierce, almost shrill, as she tried to explain to us what her family had endured during the Cultural Revolution—forced relocation, near-starvation. I could sense the brutal dissonance she was experiencing, her need to emphasize the reality of her past as she found herself in these surreal surroundings, a homey place across the world from the home she might never be able to return to. The crack in her composure only made me admire her more. She brought a breath of the world to our house, an air of significance.

The people who traveled through our dining room because of Toshi tended to do that—suggest something beyond our hectic routine out there in the woods, where we typically cycled through the same faces and places week after week, year after year.

My uncle visited us when Toshi had established himself outside our home, but still in our town. Physically, Morris resembled a shorter and clean-shaven version of my own father, and the familiar aspects of this unfamiliar person created an off-balance curiosity within me, a sense I still associate with extended family. My uncle was a practicing Buddhist, and he had an air of equanimity—in my memories he's always wearing the same slight smile—but he carried tension with him into the house. Perhaps it came from the pressure of everyone else wearing that same slight smile, too, even if they felt something other than the mild acceptance it suggested. Decades later, my father told me how anxious Toshi became in his father's presence, but I had intuited that even as a child.

One morning at breakfast my uncle asked me if I'd like to hear some Japanese poetry. I said yes, of course—I don't recall my exact age, but I was old enough to be polite, probably even old enough to want to broaden my horizons. He took a breath, fixed his eyes on mine, and let out a loud, long, undulating tone in a pitch I'd never heard before, then moved into something I could recognize as neither poem, song, nor chant but only as *weird*. I struggled to contain my embarrassed laughter. My little brother peeked his head in the room, a stricken expression on his face, and then fled. There was a split-second pause, just long enough for me to quit holding my breath and begin congratulating myself on winning the contest of composure. But no, my uncle was not finished; he was just inhaling deeply to hold another long warbling note that led to another verse. And then there was another. And another. And more. His eyes never wandered from mine. He seemed scarcely to blink. My urge to laugh waxed and waned, but I managed not to succumb to hysterics, even when my face felt like it was going to break. Finally, it was over. My uncle, with his little smile and measured voice, explained to me in some detail what I had just heard. He may have mentioned the occasions when the poem was sung, its meaning, its historical origins, I don't know. I was waiting for the kind of bridge-building comment my parents would have been likely to make, some acknowledgement that to a child raised in Pennsylvania the long chant must have appeared strange in the extreme, but it didn't come.

"That's interesting," I said when he ended his explanation. I forced an extra bit of *umph* into my pasted-on smile and retreated to my room.

At another point when Toshi was no longer sleeping at our house but when I was still quite young, his mother, Chiyo, came to our home for an afternoon, visiting from out of state. Before her arrival, the air of an occasion was evident, as well as the strain. And then there she was, the same petite woman whose image I had admired in my grandparent's stairwell, but now quite American in appearance. Instead of boasting ivory sticks and combs, her black hair was cut short and styled like Dorothy Hamill's. She wore a rabbit fur jacket, tight jeans, and heeled boots. She spoke very softly. We all sat properly in the living room as my parents made polite inquiries. After a decent interval they suggested—as they'd prepped Toshi they would—that mother and son might like to take a walk in the woods across the street to have some time together.

As soon as they left I went to get my friend down the street, and we followed, spying. We saw them from a distance, on the other side of the field where we sometimes played kickball. They looked like a couple: Toshi taller, bent towards his delicate companion almost protectively; two handsome, sleek people in a clearing in the woods, dappled in yellow-green light.

Where did she come from that day? She must have driven. Our town was near nothing. The closest airport was two hours away. She did not sleep at our house. She did not, to my recollection, even take Toshi out for a meal. What did they say to each other in the woods? What did anyone ever say about the past? Even when he was thrown out of his father's home, when he ran away from ours, Toshi was not given to—or taken in by—his mother. "She doesn't have much money," I recall my father saying. "She lives in just one room."

he night before I left Philadelphia with Carl, Reba and I climbed out her attic skylight to sit on the roof together. Aflutter with nervous excitement, I made profanity-laden proclamations, I sang my exaltation, I swung the cock of my bravado. I would not have let myself be so unmeasured with anyone else. Reba laughed with me. She witnessed my fire, this moment on a precipice I measured as greater than any before. Sex? Everyone has sex. College? Everyone had always known I'd go to college. Hitching across the country was, for me, the bold leap. We let each other go.

The goal for our first day was to cross Pennsylvania and make it to my hometown to visit my parents. We took a bus out to the suburbs, hiked around the mall parking lot to figure out which on-ramp headed in the right direction, and relieved ourselves in some bushes before we stuck out our sign, the only pedestrians in this landscape.

Whoosh. Whoosh. Whoosh. What if that was as far as we got? But a pickup truck pulled over. A miracle, every time. And a risk. Whose world were we about to enter? The first driver had a goatee. He was a recently retired trucker, and he gave us advice: watch out for truckers on speed, there were way too many of them because of the way the companies were compensating mileage. I should not have worn the shirt I had on, I should cover up a little bit more, because yeah, some of them were looking to score. But together, he concluded, we should be okay. He radioed ahead and found a trucker going our way, and the two of them arranged a hand-off.

"This guy's all right!" he told us as we approached the semi that had pulled over to receive us. He was excited by our voyage, gave a whoop as we opened the door to the highway's roar. "Good luck!" A few hours later, my dad picked us up at the interchange of I-79 and I-80.

In the two months I'd been in Philadelphia, my mom and dad had decided to separate after years of struggling in their marriage. My mom had just moved out to live in a couple of rooms in a friend's apartment, and Carl and I were going to be staying there instead of the house I grew up in. I can't remember if I made that arrangement to display daughterly loyalty, or if it was made for me because Toshi was in town and there wasn't room for Carl and me in our small family home. Either way, my cousin and I crossed paths on my mom's new porch as he was carrying in a box for her, and we exchanged terse *heys*. I mumbled an introduction, and he and Carl exchanged even terser *heys*, in that way men do when they're measuring each other up.

"You seem tense around your cousin," Carl said later.

"Do I? Maybe. He lived with us for a couple years when I was little, and he molested me a bunch," I said.

"I knew it!" Carl replied. "I knew there was something! I can always tell."

THE STORY was such a common one among those West Philly folks. Or just among folks, actually. But at the time I still presumed there was a class divide, that all manner of incest and abuse was much more common among those who grew up in cramped apartments and in trailer parks, as Carl had. When I looked at my feet as Toshi walked by on the porch that day, I was aware that I was pantomiming awkwardness and resentment at least as much as I was feeling it. I wanted to create the opportunity for Carl to call me out, because in the context of that relationship and that summer, I was almost proud of having been molested.

It was 1988, and *The Courage to Heal: A Guide for Women Survivors of Child Sexual Abuse* had recently been published. Written by Ellen Bass and Laura Davis, it was a massive bestseller, and although I wasn't aware of the book yet, its precepts permeated the culture, bringing the sexual violation of children further out of the shadows and focusing on victims' perspectives. My own abuse was starting to seem like a streetwise badge, a way to demonstrate the distance between me and the clean college girls from good homes for whom the crew from Philly had such withering scorn—or even to narrow the categorical gap between the two groups, adjoin them under the heading of done-to, woman. But to confess the assault outright would have been to make too big a deal of it. Toshi was only a cousin, after all. Not a figure of authority. Full-grown physically, maybe, when it happened, but not at the time a real, true man. And he hadn't raped me, hadn't fucked me. The horror I experienced was nowhere near as definitive as in the novels I had read or the news stories that had become common.

Still, if I downplayed the situation adequately, I could lay my hand on the mantle of victimhood. I wasn't *only* one of the lucky ones. I could, like Kathy Acker and Andrea Dworkin and the legion of smart-girl strippers, turn the situation on its head and claim strength from it, or at least a righteous knowledge. At the very least, but most importantly, I could escape the accusation of naïveté.

This would become an element to cling to as the dynamic between Carl and me continued to sharpen. On the road, the dominant storyline was that he was my guide into the world's underbelly, and it was his duty to protect my niceness, my innocence. Meanwhile, part of my education was to absorb his badness, his pain. That a nasty thing had happened to me, too, helped diffuse this frustrating dichotomy. It allowed us to sometimes step outside of it and recognize in each other those elements that others had not always seen in us, but which we'd felt: my dirtiness, of which my victimhood was a part; his vulnerability and outsized capacity for empathy, which could make the world seem like too much for him, even as he was seen by it as a menace.

W hen Toshi came back to stay with us during his leaves, he
was asked to pitch in, mostly as a reassurance that he was indeed part of the
family despite the lingering question of where he belonged. As he had when
he'd lived with us, he'd perform the after-dinner chores of scraping off plates
and sweeping the floor. Once my brother and I were older and had places to
go, he was also asked to drive us. During his visit the fall of my eighth-grade
year, he was assigned to take me to a party I'd been invited to—one where I
knew that there'd be making out. I'd been counting down the days.

A couple weeks earlier, I'd French kissed for the first time, with my curly-
haired boyfriend Jerry in a vinyl recliner in my friend's basement rec room,
her parents out and her boyfriend there, too. They had a big wet bar in that
room that we often dipped into, and I would guess we'd done so that evening,
but I was not so well looped as to preclude the dumbstruck shock I felt at
someone's cushioned lips opening my own to slip in his tongue. I don't know
for how many minutes I responded as a gaped-mouth corpse—two? twenty?

Jerry and I had been flirting with each other all summer. He'd been on
a basketball team my dad coached the year before, and he'd walk the long

walk from his grandmother's house to ours, ostensibly to shoot baskets with my brother, but then on less and less of a pretense. We spent afternoons together, and something draped between us, a weighted velvet cord, satisfyingly heavy, that we each held one end of. Desire, I suppose this was, though there was no pressure behind it until school started and boys and girls were publically paired off to play in the officiated baseball game: first base, second base, third, home run. The point is, I liked and desired him by the time we were assigned to step up to bat, and he was not only an excellent kisser, but patient.

How did he know that if he kept gently but firmly swirling his tongue, pulling it out for some lips-only nudges and then slipping it again, just a little bit farther, that I'd waken? Only thirteen years old, but his instinct was right. Even as I remained petrified, I knew I didn't want him to stop, and his refusal to read rejection in my rigor mortis mouth and frozen limbs came across as sensitive and kind rather than brutishly obtuse, until awaken I did, in a rush of heat and relief and gratitude. By the end of the evening I had fully entered the thick air and heat of sensuality.

I left the rec room with a bullish enthusiasm about sex that became a fixed part of my identity for the next two decades. What that meant in eighth grade was that I couldn't wait to make out again. I knew I'd get a chance to at the party, where my boyfriend was invited, too. The host had been talking all week, with winks and leers, about the supply room where couples could get some privacy.

DAN BUNDT'S PARENTS had more money than most, and lived in a big house on some rolling acres of land at the opposite end of the spread-out school district from my own. It'd be a long drive. My mother had walked out of the house with Toshi and me, still giving him directions when I got into the back seat of our family's Ford Fairmont station wagon.

"You're going to sit back there?" she said. "Why would you do that? Don't make him feel like a chauffer."

"This is where I want to sit," I said. I was sullen, pulled into myself and as far away from these two as I could be. This wasn't particularly for Toshi's benefit. It was a common mode of mine at the time, especially around my mother, who was less adept at sidestepping my moods than my dad, or less willing to do so.

"Come on, join me up front," Toshi added, stiffly cajoling. I just turned my head as if already watching scenery roll past. I sometimes noticed attempts of his to acknowledge me as a teenager now, to try to connect with me there, but it was awkward. In my whole life, I remember one moment of feeling comfortable with him. It occurred a few years earlier, when he was back on another visit. He had teased me about my gross habit of chewing ice cubes and regurgitating the shards back into the glass before waiting a few minutes to eat them.

"Didn't you ever eat ice cubes when you were a kid?" I said cheerfully.

"Yeah, but I didn't spit them out and eat them again!"

Something about his stated disgust and my imperviousness to it seemed bright and normal. I distinctly recall the happiness at owning the status as child.

That's not how I felt in the car that evening. We said nothing as we rounded the wooded bend that marked the border of our little settlement, then headed down the straightaway that passed through a field of milkweeds and goldenrod and led to 5th Ward, the run-down neighborhood where my boyfriend's grandmother lived. From there, we took a bridge over a creek and a train yard into town. There were streetlamps on this part of the route, and from where I sat, I could see Toshi's jaw twitch.

"What do you do at a party when you're thirteen?" he asked. "Do you make out?"

"Maybe," I said. An adult would never have asked that question. Not in that tone. This realization made me feel especially superior. I remember what I was wearing. I'd been planning it all week: rose colored corduroy knickerbockers, a white nylon blouse, and a blue quilted vest spotted with rose-colored flowers. My forelocks were pulled back on each side with small rubber bands instead of barrettes, a style I was trying after seeing it on the TV show *Mork and Mindy*.

Finally, Dan Bundt's estate-like white house appeared on a rise ahead,

"I'll be back here at ten," Toshi said.

I slammed the door.

THE BASEMENT WAS FINISHED except for the supply room, a rectangular space that smelled of the plywood shelves on the wall. We mounded up our coats under the lowest shelves to make nests. Dan Bundt had a smirk on his face the whole night. I don't remember who he took back there. I remember how necessary it felt to be supine, the way my whole body responded to the oceanic kissing. My nylon blouse came untucked, and Jerry's hands ran up my bare back, and I felt like I was rolling in satin sheets—the existence of which I had recently become aware. Other couples giggled and whispered and clomped in and out of the room. We stayed in the closet, emerging only once for some orange pop, retreating quickly from the boisterousness back to our den. His hands roamed wider, slid along just the sides of my bra, still a cupless child's model, the white triangles overlaid with a pilled lace.

At ten o'clock, Dan's parents called us up to wait for our rides on the front lawn. Spotlights shone up from the ground to illuminate the barn-shaped garage that featured an asphalt basketball court. Some of the boys played but mine stayed by me. He radiated the cracked-open tenderness I would later come to recognize as heralding the possibility of love.

"Was it fun?" Toshi asked me insinuatingly when we were out the driveway and back onto dark road.

"Yes," I said.

I wasn't afraid to be alone with him. It's easy to ascribe in retrospect a consciousness that might not have quite been there, but the sense memory of being in that car is very strong. I think I felt smug. I think I felt that I had pushed off, gained a knowledge and a power that put me beyond him now, and that he knew it, too. And he had to drive me. His assigned role was chauffeur, servant, and I'd keep going further, beyond and beyond in a float of physical bliss he hadn't given me and wasn't privy to.

OUR TOWN was about ninety-five percent white. The other five percent of the population was almost entirely African American. Jerry was biracial. By the time of this party, my social circle had tacitly agreed to accept us as couple, but the rest of our world didn't, and as we became more of a public item, judgment rained down on us, hard, from both sides of the race line. A group of black girls started harassing me They'd corner me in the bathroom and make threats, or find me after school and follow me while I walked. One day, the group caught up with me on my way to watch my boyfriend's basketball game, and the ringleader hit me in the face. Her fist toppled my scoop of mint chocolate chip ice cream before meeting my cheekbone. Our respective friends had seemed to recede in the moment of contact, but then they were back again, hers moving her off noisily as she continued to shout threats into the air, mine clustering around me hennishly, "Are you okay? Are you okay? Are you okay?"

Eventually we made it to the school where the game was being played. It was already third quarter, and I was surrounded by a security detail of big-haired thirteen-year-old white girls. After the game I told Jerry what had happened. "You've got to tell them to stop," I demanded.

He had his foot on a chair. He looked the other way. "I'll talk to my cousin," he said.

In the summer when we'd walked together along the rural route I lived on, occasionally we'd hear an epitaph thrown from a passing car, denigrating me for my affection for him, and by extension him for being who he was, for existing at all. It was easy enough for me to ignore this, the cars going fast and the words dying out quickly on the wind, replaced by the bird chirps and locust buzz. But one day as we walked through his grandmother's more populated neighborhood, a full can of pop was thrown at us with the slur. It exploded in front of us at the foot of the bridge into town. When the school year started, most socializing occurred at high school football games and then at indoor basketball games, where walking in front of the bleachers meant being put on display. This was the main point of the events for my friends and me, the thrill, the performance for which we so carefully chose our outfits. But when I walked to the concession stand with him, the nudges and disapproving stares were as palpable as knocks on our shoulders. He did not turn to me demanding that I call off the snarling white people, that I do something about this. He absorbed it. I could see the cost on his face.

He'd been known for being hot-tempered and brooding and prone to bluffing, but not so much with me, until now. The emotional terrain between us got rockier. He got in trouble for fighting at school. As the tensions mounted, I became frantic. "But his mom is white! His mom is white!" I would cry to my friends. Even by the stupid logic of segregation it made no sense to me why he couldn't hold hands with someone who shared a skin tone with his own mother. I thrashed at the bind he was in, at the blazing injustice. But I perceived my friends growing weary of my struggle. They didn't care what the color of his skin was, but they wanted the drama in our life to come from who was rounding what base with whom; they wanted the hot glare of new attention on us to be flattering, a signifier of our just-hatched cuteness and sexual viability, not of transgression. And word was spreading. He and I were the objects of dinner table talk, of grocery store gossip. Finally my best friend's parents told her she could no longer hang out with me outside of school if I continued seeing him. As disgusted as I was with it, this absolute came as almost a relief by that time, during the darkest days of the year. In a hectic flurry, I broke up with him. I swallowed the hatred I felt for my town and aligned with the demands of the mob and the pack.

The next boy I coupled up with, a tall, pale, laconic blond, wasn't nearly as good a kisser. In fact, I felt repulsed by his slick squirmy tongue. We didn't last long, and I had no designated partner for the first make-out party of spring. In the back and forth matchmaking that took up the first hour of the festivity, two boys emerged as possibilities. They each took their turn before me for an interview. One I had "dated" a year ago, before I was ready to French kiss. He had a swoop of ginger hair and a wide sheepish smile, and he displayed some self-awareness of the ridiculous situation we were in. We probably could have been real friends. The other was a huge wrestler named Tad, who had a helmet of curly hair, a cleft chin, bowed lips. He was as handsome as a cartoon Achilles, and insistent, full-in. "I want to go with you," he said, the term we used to officiate regular mashing.

"Okay, you guys. Lights out in five minutes!" hollered the hostess, flicking at the switch to warn us the main event was about to begin. We didn't always have the luxury of Dan Bundt's well-appointed home. This evening we were in a more typical basement, one big room with some rugs laid over the cement floor, a play space defined by an overflowing chest of toys and a child-sized table set now with potato chips and dip, a laundry area with a rusted utility sink, and a section with a wall of shelves lined with jars of homemade jam and put-up beans. There were no separate chambers in which to find privacy, so anyone who didn't have a partner would just be sitting in the gloom once the lights went out, waiting while the rest of us groped. I chose the wrestler and we took a spot against the wall.

At first I liked the feel of his big body subsuming mine. His kisses were wide-mouthed and hard, but not unpleasant. Returning them was a bit like playing pinball: I had to be quick and rough to keep up, and the whiz-bang pumped me full of adrenaline. But the game sped up too quickly when Tad began using his hands. He didn't bother with my upper half. His palm kept zooming down the back of my gaping jeans. I kept reaching behind me and pulling it out. This happened again and again, again, and again. I couldn't concentrate on the kissing. I tried to squirm free, to at least change position to better guard the entries to my clothing, but he had me pinned. Our size differential was no longer hot. I don't recall whether I verbally said no to him; I might have in a whisper, "Don't" or "not now," or "not that," but it didn't occur to me to make a scene. Finally what I did was go limp and let him. His forearm rested in the crack of my buttocks and his wrist at my asshole and his finger went into my vagina and squiggled. It felt like nothing much. A mild discomfort. I was above myself, and miserable, and bored.

I sprung away when the lights went up, went right for the chips. Tad came to stand beside me, and I turned my back on him. He came to stand beside me again while we waited outside for our parents to come, and I looked over his shoulder. "I'll call you tomorrow," he said. I shrugged. He said something else and I turned away. When he did call, and I was cold to him, I could hear the confusion in his voice, and I was astounded that he didn't get it, that he'd think I'd want to replay the scene from the basement ever again. But I certainly didn't verbalize why I was spurning him, not even to my friends.

MOST OF MY MEMORIES of eighth grade are tinted a melancholy shade of grey—the racism, my complicity in it, some bouts of ugly drinking, the meanness of some peers. But I learned things that year. There was sexual pleasure to be had out there, but my having found it, having reached pubescence, didn't preclude the bad sex stuff, the getting trapped and tricked. I had status if I played by the racist rules, but even then I remained vulnerable too.

Both the rules and the vulnerability made me grim and steely. I developed more wiles. I took the remove I employed during an act of invasion and fashioned a shield with it to be held up before contact occurred, to be let down only sparingly as I moved through the crowds and deeper into the world of men and boys. Hitchhiking was not the first or last decision I made to put myself in a dodgy situation, but I always went with my guard up, with my defenses arrayed—Carl among them. And sometimes, years into what did often feel like a war between the sexes—with each side trying to get what they wanted without having things taken against their will—I'd sit in my tent and sharpen my sword on those two, on Toshi and the wrestler. I was ready to slice those motherfuckers, if I met their ilk again. But I appreciated my experiences with them too, in a way, for showing me at a young age what was out there, that I might have to suit up, and that I could.

RESEARCH SHOWS:
ONE OUT OF FIVE

S ince I was a child, I had a sense of myself as fortunate both in terms of security and circumstance, and this sense was not extinguished by my awareness of sexual vulnerability. But how fortunate? What was normal? Where did my family and I fit in the world? I wanted the big picture, and I kept my eyes open looking for clues, eavesdropped whenever I could. And I read—first only books, indiscriminately and voraciously, but as I entered my teen years, my father's newspapers and magazines, too—*Newsweek, The New York Times, Harper's, The Nation, The New Criterion, The New York Review of Books.*

The habit remains, as does the simple curiosity, although now I'm aware of other motives. I want to situate myself in order to combat self-pity, inform my opinions, and challenge my perspective, especially as I've settled into a groove alongside many people who were born affluent and remain so. In this quest, the anecdotal and narrative don't seem sufficient, drawn though I am to them. Now when I'm wrestling with how I think or feel about a topic, I also read studies and statistics, almost always online. Often I glom on to the overly simplified type designed for easy digestion by laypeople. *One out of three people. One out of four women. One out of five Americans.* It's either a lot or a few, depending on what you're talking about.

One out of four children in the United States is being raised, like Carl was, by a single parent.

More than one out of five children live in families, as Carl did at times, with incomes below the federal poverty limit.

One out of five children will be sexually abused.

One out of three children sexually abused will have been the victim of a relative.

One out of three Americans has a college degree.

One out of four female college students will be sexually assaulted.

One out of four Americans has a criminal record.

One in five children and adolescents are affected by mental health problems.

DURING MY ADOLESCENCE, as boys my own age showed interest in my genitals as Toshi had done, and on into my adulthood, I told myself that Toshi probably molested me as a way of experimenting with techniques in order to please girls his own age. This explanation answered some of my questions about what had happened, and why, and it fit our culture's notion that teenaged boys are incessantly horny. But in one of my sporadic searches on the subject several years after I learned that Toshi had been arrested for sexual abuse as an adult, I discovered that pedophilia is classified as a psychiatric disorder, and adolescents over the age of sixteen who take a sexual interest in prepubescent children are considered pedophiles. This devastated me—the seriousness of that word, the implications of it, that I had been a victim of it, and that I had not done anything to stop it. But the taboo suggested by the term also validated my continued troubled interest in what I sometimes felt should have been a minor strand in my life.

I n addition to his height and road smarts and excellent dick, perhaps I'd chosen to travel with Carl because I guessed he was someone who'd say, "I knew it!" when I told him about my sex abuse, instead of, "Did you tell your parents?" Someone who wouldn't see me as damaged—if indeed that's what I was—and who might even like what damage he found. Someone who could, being so familiar, point it out to me, press his fingers into the bruise, help me find its exact dimensions—to find the sources of pleasure within the pain.

I'd been told, or maybe I just assumed—based on the word *sex*, and novels that reveled in the legacy of incest, and the increasing awareness in American society about childhood sexual abuse, and the way such abuse figured into the plot of *The Color Purple*, one of my favorite books—that damage should be there, but I still wasn't quite sure what to look for. I wasn't quite sure whether I qualified.

WHAT WERE MY PARENTS thinking that summer when I passed through their divided doorstep with a huge, sulking man, a half-baked plan to hitchhike, and fifty dollars in my pocket? After twenty years of focusing on their children, they were thinking of themselves, probably; their lives were upended that season. Also they were thinking of my younger brother, who was acting out—raging, throwing things, maybe involved with drugs.

I'm now raising my own kids in a community where many parents play an integral part in planning their college-aged children's summers—travel opportunities, internships, intensive workshops in baroque instruments. But in 1988 my mom and dad were probably thinking—correctly—that I could take care of myself, and that they couldn't have stopped me, even if they'd thought it best.

MY COUSIN WAS TASKED with giving Carl and me a ride out of town and dropping us at the I-80 interchange. Carl sat in the passenger seat and emanated a bristling reticence that I assumed was on my behalf. I sat in the middle of the back seat, unsure whether to mirror Carl's attitude, as I felt he expected me to do, or maintain small talk to put the two men at ease.

"Didn't you hitchhike when you were young?" I asked Toshi, finally. I had a vague memory of him hitching with his friend Dan, an affable, denim-clad, stoner-type who was at our house often, slapping us five, laying down the seventies slang that made my mom laugh and want to give it a try. "Dan The Man," she started to call him. We all did. "Cool, man," she started to say, half sarcastically, half pleadingly. I was born in 1968, and it had always seemed to me like it must have been a difficult time to become a mother, trapped between expectations of the more conservative past and the freewheeling present. Toshi and Dan *were* the seventies to me, with their hanks of chin-length hair, their aviator glasses, their thumbs in their belt loops.

But now it was the late eighties and Toshi didn't have much to offer about hitchhiking, aside from a rueful, "Yeah, maybe." A sentence or two in response to my questions, and then he went back to silence, the muscles in his square jaw rippling. I sat back in my seat until it was time to discuss where he should let us out.

In comparison, conversation with the trucker who picked us up was easy. We jumped out of his cab at dusk by an exit on the Ohio turnpike. It was to be our first night in the open, and the exurban American landscape spread before me with the formidable majesty of a young mountain range—the midsummer grass was crunchy and scorched, the clutch of utilitarian businesses emitted a neon hiss, the gas station sign held aloft by towering white poles vibrated faintly from the never-ceasing traffic.

My heart rose and sank. We stood without speaking; I was waiting for Carl to direct us.

"Walking around with these packs makes us a mark," Carl said. "I'm going to park you with them in those bushes while I look around for a place to sleep."

The phrase "park you" rankled me, but I hadn't even thought about being a mark. This was a survival game now, and shutting up about semantics seemed expedient. I waited obediently, sat among a grove of hemlocks, the spiny brown ground cover and ruby berries familiar to me from my childhood, when I whiled away hours in the neighbor's hedges.

Carl came back from his recognizance excited to have found an old, empty dining car on an unattached piece of rail track. "It's a perfect place for us to sleep. There's some bushes planted around it so it's mostly protected, but it's real clean under there. No one's been using it."

This paradise was nearby, but nothing seems near when you're on foot with your possessions strapped to your back, walking in an environment designed for cars. There was just enough room under the boxcar for us to crawl. We made our camp there before the purple light had a chance to turn black, laying out the single sleeping mat in the gravel between the two rails, fishing out our toothbrushes. When we emerged without our heavy packs and were able to stand straight, it was as if we were stepping out in finery to go on a special-occasion date.

We ate dinner at the chain pancake restaurant next to the gas station. We'd spent one day hoboing, and already, being waited on felt like a masquerade. When we returned to our abandoned dining car, we managed to have sex, Carl's elbows grinding into the rocks as he thrust into me from the unaccustomed horizontal angle, my face smashed to one side against his chest, my hand on the hump of his back to protect it from scraping against the metal beam just above us. The claustrophobia was both oppressive and erotic.

Afterward, we created an Armageddon scenario in whispers—what would we do to survive when civilization crumbled, when ruins from the industrialized past were all that was left. I felt intoxicated with the sense that I was living an aesthetic and thus proving it to be more than that, fulfilling some wild and lonely hunger to be real.

OUR SLEEPING ACCOMMODATIONS were different each night or two—we crashed among boxes in a warehouse run by anarchists, under train trestles, in break winds, public parks, strangers' floors, and on the slopes of mountains near peaks that yielded spectacular 360-degree views. Wherever we were— however hot or cold or secluded or not— we managed to fuck ferociously.

After the first couple days of traveling, we fought that way, too—although perhaps "fought" is not the correct term to use. We exploded, we surfed each other's moods. Well, Carl mostly exploded, and I mostly surfed. He took his role as leader of the expedition seriously, and he was alternately critical of my blitheness and inexperience and hyper-protective of me; he saw himself as the only thing preventing me from being raped at every turn.

One day, after I wandered off while he napped in a park, he became enraged. He hollered and screamed—didn't I know what could happen to me?— and threatened to put me on a bus back home. He hollered and screamed other times, too, at me or at the air, and he could also become ominously silent, transmitting punishment in the adjustment of his stride or wherever he directed his gaze. I had not seen the full extent of his darkness in Philadelphia, where we had breaks from each other, and where we were on—although I did not know it at the time—our best behavior. Now we were together ceaselessly, and our every contradiction was laid bare, every defense down.

I began to realize that the danger of me being raped consumed Carl not only because he was concerned for my safety, but also because he was troubled by his own bifurcated responses to the images of my sexual assault. "I had a bad dream," he whispered to me one night in the tent, waking up with a hard-on. "There were truckers. Fat, ugly guys. Big beards. One guy was holding your arms. And you, you didn't like it."

My own response was bifurcated, too. We rolled toward each other after his confession. The sex had only gotten better on our trip. I was staggered by dopamine. But my concern about the way Carl viewed me and treated me off the sleeping mat grew.

To make sense of the situation I found myself in, to contain the constant stream of thrill and strangeness, exaltation and estrangement, to keep a grasp of my very sanity it seemed, at times—after all, I was underfed, under-slept, over-stimulated in every way even if often blindingly bored—I wrote in my journal. Carl had a notebook, too, in which he would sketch, occasion-ally, but it didn't hold his attention the way writing held mine. And when I wrote, he felt left out, which was dangerous. I began to do it furtively.

One night we were bickering, and I walked away to relieve myself and then took a stroll around the neighborhood nearby the arroyo where we were camping. I returned to our spot to find Carl holding my notebook, his face contorted over something I'd written, his eyes full of tears. Some long min-utes into his ensuing tirade, I gathered that a sentence or two had confirmed his suspicion that I didn't love him, that I was only using him and was bound to leave him for my previous boyfriend. That I was slumming. He railed in rage and pain. I tried to calm him; there was no room for me to express my indignation about my violated journal. We ended up making up enough to cuddle to sleep on an aqueduct ledge where we had made our bed, his head in my arms as huge and archetypal as an Easter Island statue, but things still felt shaky in the morning. I voiced my concerns about privacy, and Carl was rueful, but for both of us, anger and mistrust lingered.

This was our state when we made a miscalculation about where to hop off our first ride. We found ourselves away from the main highway and on the Grand Junction business route, where we knew it'd be difficult to get a lift because most people were likely traveling locally. Hot, hungry, grouchy, holding a cardboard sign that said "Salt Lake City," we walked on the com-mercial strip for what seemed like hours, past oil-change garages and fast food restaurants and the endless parking lots of strip malls. Finally, a rat-trap pickup pulled over. There were two guys in the front seat, more in the open bed. The driver, stringy dark hair hanging beneath a spattered cap, said they were only going a little ways, and it was dirty back there, but they could get us to the highway if we wanted to hop in. We'd already decided what we would do if we were offered a scenario like this, outnumbered by men: we'd turn it down. But the driver revved the engine in our moment's pause, and we were desperate and surly. We climbed in the bed of the pickup.

I flopped my pack down, grateful and relieved. And then I realized what they had meant by "dirty." It was a roofer's truck. Everything—the ladders, the buckets, the tarps, the three glint-eyed guys sitting with their backs to the cab—was covered in tar. As we rattled out of the business district and back toward the real highway, I lifted my pack slowly—a cobweb of gooey black tar, like a giant's wad of licorice gum, stretched from the pack to the truckbed. Everything lashed to it—the sleeping mat, the extra clothes—was covered.

Carl yanked the pack toward himself. His hands grew black as he examined the damage, clearly furious with me. He grabbed my arm with both hands and rubbed the tar into my skin, as if he was wringing out a rag. He grabbed my other arm and did the same. The roofers laughed roughly, enjoying the show. Carl was playing to them. My understanding of the nature of my vulnerability as the lone female in the truck shifted; this was no longer the story of the girl as fuckable rape bait. This was the woman as object of derision, as kicking post.

Carl screamed at me for ruining his gear and the men watched, chuckled. I had reached a nadir. I was watching my own subjugation. When the truck slowed to let us off, Carl threw my pack into the dirt and pushed me after it.

The silver lining was this: if I was going to be shoved off a truck with a pack covered in wet tar, little cash of my own, and an enraged man my only acquaintance in a thousand miles, this was an ideal spot for it to happen. There was a small rest stop within walking distance. I spied a KOA campground just beyond that, dotted with RVs. Surely someone there would be able to help me if Carl refused to travel further with me, or if he became violent. I formulated alternative scenarios in the hour that I spent bent over the bathroom sink. Each one of them assumed the kindness of married Caucasian strangers toward a lone Caucasian girl and the stalwartness of my parents, resources I could take fuller advantage of if I wasn't tethered to Carl. The liability of my gender could become an asset. My relative ease in polite society could be a benefit, rather than something about which to feel guilty.

As it turned out, Carl was calm and contrite when I emerged from the restroom, which left me somewhere between relieved and disappointed. We spent the night in the campground, humbled enough by our debacle to pay the fee to sleep fear-free and have access to showers and utility sinks. To further comfort ourselves, we ordered a pizza from the menu tacked up on a bulletin board rather than cooking our usual lentils over a fire.

And we opened ourselves up to acquaintanceship. We sat around the campfire of a friendly couple with an RV who were fascinated by our adventure. They had extra retractable chairs, and it felt luxurious to sink into one, especially with my hair still damp from the shower, my belly full, and my skin feeling crispy and clean. Carl and I grew expansive while we related our trip to them. We liked how we appeared in their eyes. We became a team again, taking turns highlighting the adventures we'd had and down-playing the misery.

"I'd love to have done something like that when I was younger," the woman said when we'd paused.

"You think so?" her husband asked, noticeably surprised.

"I know so." She had a dreamy, resolute expression on her plain face. I liked her very much. I liked the kinship I felt with these campers. I saw them now as fellow adventurers, when just that morning I would have dismissed them as the type of bloated Americans with whom I was at war. And basking in their attention made me feel lucky again. The fine dust of the campground that was settling on my skin felt like talc. The cool, fresh air that I breathed when I turned my face from the fire seemed to smooth and polish the inside of my skull. Even with my deepened understanding of my compromised position, I felt happy and proud that I was the rare woman going for broke on the road.

THERE WERE MORE indignities in our final leg to the West Coast, and when the sun turned the Green River golden, when we tore the sheets off a Motel 6 in Reno before walking out into the neon night, when we woke up along the American River while the early morning sun hit the canyon walls, I felt I had earned the magic with my forbearance of the muck. Our third-to-last ride, gotten around Sacramento, was from some teenaged boys, who piled into the front seat of a sedan that almost certainly belonged to one of their fathers so we could have the back. They were so proud of their daring to pick up hitchhikers that they couldn't quit guffawing, sneaking peeks at us as if we were circus freaks. Our penultimate ride was with a drunk; Carl sat in the front seat and I in the back, so we couldn't even make eye contact. Vodka bottles clanked in the foot wells, but we only had an hour or so to go with him. He got us to Berkeley.

Our final ride to San Francisco was procured for us by a mime who had seen us walking along the asphalt with our packs. He urged us toward the casual carpool spot and made it his business to pair us with a vehicle heading over the Bay Bridge. He jumped about in the street in his black and white clown costume while we stood by a sign instructing passengers of the protocols: *fasten your seatbelt, don't eat in the vehicle, let the driver initiate conversation or not.* It wasn't long before a car pulled over for us. We were one short ride away from the beacon of the Beats, a place both of us had read about for years but had never seen. Sometimes we weren't a man and a woman, a girl and a boy, two people tussling over who was being used or abused. Instead, we were friends. Before we walked to the passenger-side door the mime was holding open, we looked at each other and laughed out loud.

A lthough I was only four when it began, the memories I have of being sexually abused by Toshi are vivid. I perceive myself to be watching and rewatching certain moments as if I had caught them on video; they feature the too-close perspective and shaky camera work common to clips captured by a small child who's grabbed her parent's phone, the amplified breath and over-loud whispers of a microphone placed too close to a mouth.

I know that the vividness of recollections is no guarantee of their accuracy, and that every memory—even one from last week—is more of an always-changing reconstruction than a playback of a recorded activity, but I've never doubted the basic facts about what happened between Toshi and me. What I'm aware of being unsure about is the order of certain events. There are two recollections in particular that I'm conscious of trying to stitch together chronologically. I'm not positive the one incident led to the other, but it would make sense.

The first memory: Toshi was in my bed one night, and we heard a creak— the sound of the door opening at the foot of the stairs. I could feel him stiffen. He lifted off me as he pushed himself into a chaturanga, a half push-up. I immediately felt cooler as air filled the new space between his body and mine, but I lay just as still as I had been, waiting, as I also had been, to see what would happen next, with no inkling that I could affect the trajectory.

There was a rustle, a soft thump—my mother, putting something in the basket she kept on the first stair—and the door closed again. Toshi's weight fell back on to me, but he was still attuned to the noises of the house, ready to react. I could sense it.

Toshi had already told me this game was a secret from my parents, but as I registered his divided attention, something dawned on me: this was not like the other secrets I kept from the adult world, a clutch of stolen M&Ms, or a vulnerability that would elicit condescension or teasing. This was a secret *from* me even as I helped keep it, and it involved more than playing a game at too late an hour. The contrast between Toshi's size and mine became apparent in a flash, and I intuited that his largeness was the mark of a bully in this situation, not that of the friendly big-brother figure my mom had been hoping he'd be, that I'd been primed to see him as even if this game was strange. *He* would be the one to get in trouble if my parents heard us, not me. End of memory.

The second memory: one night I finally said, "No. Only over the underpants." I said it loud enough that he shushed me. I could feel his muscles jump at my raised voice. I could feel his fear.

MY OWN four-year-old daughter tries on many moods and voices. She often complains with a drawn-out nasal snivel; she reverts to mispronouncing Rs and Ls when expressing both excitement and disappointment. In moments of defiance she makes her voice as loud and large and fierce as she can. I struggle to respond levelly to any of this. There are days when it makes my skin crawl, when I model the very behavior I abhor, snapping and yelling. But it's the combination of whiney, insolent baby talk that can send me into the surest rage, and that's the tone I used when I refused Toshi.

Although it's possible I've created this memory in retrospect, I swear I recognized my voice as bratty and overtly childish even on the night I first told him no. I can still hear it in my head— a flat whine, a toddler's intractability. But my words worked. His hand left my flesh. For that night, he retreated.

AND SO BEGAN a second phase of our interaction, when what transpired in my bed became more of a contest, a negotiation. He had to wheedle, he had to whine. Sometimes it seemed we were both preschoolers fighting over a toy, tugging back and forth. Other times I did not engage in the contest; I pouted, occasionally deigned to grant favors just to relieve the monotony of saying no. Eventually the control would be yanked from me, and I'd find something off or open that I had wanted covered or closed, while a hot animal panted above me. In those moments, after having been intensely—tensely—present in the negotiation, I would vacate my body, bail. But in this power play, even when I didn't win, I was a contender.

My greatest source of strength came from my confidence in my parents' love, which gave me a stability Toshi didn't have. He was sometimes given authority in our home as the big kid, the proto adult. But he was also the outsider. I sensed the separateness between us, between the collective "us" of my family, and him, alone. Unwanted. If his parents had really loved him, why had they sent him away?

Something cool emerged in me, some part that was untouchable and pleased about it—I wasn't the one sighing in frustration. I wasn't the one panting. I wasn't the one who jumped at a creak or a thud. All of the stakes seemed higher for him. Even when I lost, I could distance myself from my body. He still managed to get his hand in my underpants plenty, and more, eventually—it's hard to write about; it makes me cross my legs and cringe—but there was a different dynamic. Instead of lying mutely, uncomprehending, I was honing an arsenal. Watchful. Learning cause and effect. Using what I could.

I WASN'T EVER GLAD when my bedroom door cracked open and Toshi slipped inside my room. I did not want him in my bed. But I did not raise my voice much above a whisper, either. I was intensely interested in what transpired.

I WANTED THIS section of the book to be about how not-that-bad being sexually abused was. About the ways it was empowering, even. Because it was empowering in some ways. I want to believe that, and I do. For one thing, I became practiced in refusing someone whose breath I could feel on my skin, which would prove helpful when I was old enough to decide who to let close but no closer, and when to say no.

But that's not all. In trying to understand the impact the assault had on me, I've sometimes arrived at this: the complexity of the situation, as I saw it as a child, made me complex, or at least revealed, very early on, my inborn intricacy. What happened to me at night when I was so young gave me reason to inspect, to speculate. It taught me to wait in the dark, because there'd be a moment when shapes would become clear, even in the shadows. I learned to suspect secrets everywhere, to pry until they were revealed. In my story of myself, having been abused helped me orient myself on the path to becoming the Beat-reading adventurer that I aspired to be, that I actually was, for awhile.

And yet, when putting down these thoughts, I wrote, "One night Toshi was in my room," and then I paused as the memory came into focus. I changed the word *room* to *bed* to be more accurate, because as I remembered I could feel his weight on my single bed, the sea-like roll of the mattress, the closeness of the slanted ceiling above my head. Sitting in front of the computer, my eyes welled up with tears. The feelings came down: fear and anger and helplessness and sadness. Am I recollecting these emotions, or are they virgin, evoked by retrospective empathy?

Either way, I want to get away from them. My strokes are strong; they're moving me there, up, towards more air. But there's a tug, another flash of memory. I grimace.

This time, before pushing away from the discomfort, I offer tenderness to the little girl in her room trying to figure out the patterns of the night. No matter how she felt at the time, she shouldn't have had to do that. I send a message that she'll still be strong if no one comes to disturb her sleep. That I'll listen if she wants to tell a different story.

THE END OF A CONTINENT

In the three-plus weeks that Carl and I had been traveling, a large Philadelphia contingent had already converged on San Francisco, lured west by Joe, the house member who'd relocated earlier that year. When we arrived, a few Philly folks were crashing at his apartment, which he shared with two other women. Carl and I joined them on the floor in Joe's room.

The first time we spent an afternoon away from each other felt strange; we hadn't been apart for more than a couple hours for nearly a month. Walking about with a group of women—small-talking, intimacy sharing—made me feel light and buoyant. Those words have a positive connotation, but the sensation was not only pleasant. It smacked of irrelevancy, lack of import. I sometimes felt like a balloon tied to a child's hand, being pulled along.

One day I found myself sitting in the cold sun of Golden Gate Park with Maerene. We certainly weren't at the Bounce Babe anymore. Together we puzzled over the particular glamour and dirt of San Francisco. It was not quite what it'd seemed, glittering as it had from a distance. We didn't love the Upper Haight, which seemed a worn-down consumer parody of itself, with troops of punk kids younger than us panhandling. We were put off by the stern signs in café bathrooms that scolded people for leaving their needles in the sink. But we were here, and we agreed it was a distinctive place. The fog made us shiver, a sign that we'd reached the outer edge of the continent.

We compared our trips across the country: the rocky but relatively luxurious style of hitchhiking I'd done with Carl versus her short, hard haul hitchhiking with Deena. Every ride they'd gotten had been with a trucker; they'd covered the nearly three thousand miles in under three days, never really getting off the road.

"I didn't think it was safe to do it without a guy," I said.

"It's not, really," she replied.

They'd gotten all the way to Nebraska before a driver stopped the truck in the middle of the night in the middle of nowhere and said calmly that he didn't care who it was, but one of them was going to have sex with him or he was leaving them both on the side of the road. Maerene told me she would have gotten out, but she was glad when Deena agreed to the sex. Having been in a few semis myself now, I could picture the set-up: curtains separating a bunk from the rest of the cab. Deena and the man crawled in the back. Maerene curled up in the passenger seat. She said she heard the sex, the man grunting—it didn't take long—and then the snoring. Deena slept in the back with him. Finally Maerene'd fallen asleep lying across the seats. The trucker was going all the way to San Francisco, and Deena had sex with him again the next night, too. He bought them both dinner.

"If it were me who had to do it, I'd've gotten out," Maerene repeated in her Irish accent. I could sense her tracing the moment again in her mind, the path she had worn between points. "But I didn't tell her not to do it. I was afraid to get out. I was glad we didn't have to. I feel some responsibility. She did it for me, too."

"Have you talked to Deena about it?"

"She said it was just like another trick."

"That's probably what it was to her." Deena had worked in a brothel in Philly; one of the first to do so. Maerene had only danced, and not for long.

"I AM A GIRL, a female, always in danger of assault," wrote Sylvia Plath.

Although I sometimes enjoyed the comfort of the pack, I never fully meshed with the Philly women—Maerene was the closest I came to making a new real friend. But I recognized in many of them a response to Plath's notion, and a titillation by it, that was similar to mine. The commodification of sex, through selling or other means, was in conversation with the risk of femaleness, and not necessarily to be avoided. By consciously risking assault we could deny its punitive power. By acknowledging the sexual objectification so present in young women's lives, we engaged in a dialogue about it. Maybe we could gain something. And if the exchange was sordid, so what? Without the contrast of true squalor, the moments of transcendence wouldn't seem as holy.

What Maerene had risked, what Deena had given, the relationship it had to my own story and Carl's fears, it all added up—as so many things did to me then—to a sex-fueled story that made me want to fuck all the more. Carl and I were somewhat hindered by sharing a room with four other people, but we weren't picky. We had sex in the big hallway closet. We had sex during any score of minutes we could be alone in the bedroom. We had sex at night when we thought that the others were asleep, and even after I learned that there was a voyeur in the group who feigned slumber because he liked watching, it didn't really bother me. We weren't the only ones getting it on in that crowded apartment. Maerene hooked up with Joe, moved from the floor of his room to his bed. There was at least one night when I looked over and noticed their own sly humping, all four of us having sex at once. Who knows what the lucky voyeur was doing with himself on that evening. Still, for all our lack of fastidiousness, Carl and I missed the abandon to be had in a tent.

We hadn't been sure what was going to happen after we reached San Francisco—Carl had tentatively planned to make a claim somewhere on the coast, and he thought it might be there. But after our only real sightseeing jaunt, when we visited North Beach, home of the Beats, and wandered through City Lights bookstore, we decided to dispel the funk of the letdown by pressing on together and heading north.

Arcadia. Eugene. Portland. Welcome to the Pacific Northwest. We took a good week to get up to Seattle. Some friends of friends there hipped us to a house near their squat that had been abandoned mid-construction, and we settled in. The drywall had been put up, but it hadn't been painted. The house had no fixtures, electricity, or water. Staying there was like camping with walls.

The summer had been a long one for me because the University of Sheffield, where I was to spend my junior year, didn't start classes until October, but the chill of fall was already settling upon us. For the past three months, I'd thought about little beyond Carl and crossing the country, but I'd come as far as was possible, and in only a score or so more days, I would be crossing an ocean in the other direction. I started leaning east. It took only one scan through the newspaper's classifieds for me to find someone offering a cheap one-way airline ticket to Buffalo, New York, which was within driving distance of my hometown. My parents wired me the money, and I met the seller in the airport, trading a hundred dollars in cash for the ticket home. When the day came, I got on a plane and flew in a handful of hours over the two thousand-plus miles it'd taken us almost two months to travel together.

When I left, Carl was still trying to figure out what to do next. Back to San Francisco? Further north to Alaska? We'd been too wrapped up in the pulsing between us for his own compass to settle on a point. The money he'd saved as a laborer, which we'd padded with some cold calling in San Francisco, was almost gone, and so was his will to travel farther. Only a few days after I flew away, he decided to hitch hike back east in order to see me off to England. He wanted to find a way to come visit me there, and I was elated we'd continue our adventures together.

CARL FIGURED he could save enough money fast enough to fly to England and fund a European version of our trip by selling himself in medical studies, so once I left the country, that's what he did. As he sat in hospital beds having his blood taken and his sleep patterns or nervous response times altered with trial drugs, he'd write me long letters. They'd arrive a week or two after he'd sent them, the envelopes tattooed so heavily in red and black ink that they felt almost damp. Sometimes the Philly crew would score an illegal calling card that worked overseas, and Carl would ring the one phone in my block of flats, located in the stand-alone laundry. If the person who answered was kind enough, he or she would tape a note on the door of my unit, telling me when he was going to try to call again, and I'd go sit on a bench in the cement-block structure, trying to read as the dryers thumped, hoping the card would still be working and the payphone would remain unoccupied and that he'd remember to call. I was lonely in Sheffield, and the letters and calls meant a lot to me, but Carl's tone did not help leaven the dark winter months. "Coming to see you, bitch," he wrote on the spine of a mix tape he made for me.

"I talked to Joe last night. But things don't sound so good for him," he told me on the phone, his voice sounding almost juvenile. "I guess he and Maerene have been doing a lot of heroin. Like, a real lot. And they're doing a lot of S&M. I don't mean the fun stuff. Like, they don't even have sex." He whispered this last.

We sat in silence for a moment. The allure of a black leather belt fastened around wrists or folded over to make a nice thwack was something that we understood, but the lack of penetration was incomprehensible.

"What do they *do*?" I finally asked.

"She just ties him up and hurts him and leaves him there. And then she makes him look in a mirror while she tells him things. Bad things. Like how pathetic he is. And he says that's what he wants, that he doesn't want to have sex anymore, but he doesn't . . . He doesn't sound good."

Joe had seemed like one of the healthier members of the Philly tribe. His calves were strong from bike riding. He didn't smoke cigarettes. The apartment he'd been living in was neat.

"Have you talked to anyone who's out there?"

"Yeah, I talked to Mel," Carl said. "And he says it's true. He says they're pretty much just flat-out junkies, but worse, because they don't know how to do it, like Lisa and them do. They don't know how to maintain. I half think I should use this money and go out and get him. But what could I do?"

I'D EARNED ENOUGH college credits in high school so that I could skip the last quarter of the year in Sheffield. I completed my coursework in April, and Carl had reached the financial finish line in time. He flew into Heathrow with his backpack and the daypack I'd be carrying once again as mine.

But the gloomy news about Joe and Maerene was representative of the dark cloud surrounding us. We hadn't realized that springtime in England and northern Europe would be so cold and rainy. We hadn't thought through the fact that although hitchhiking might be more acceptable in Europe, people didn't speak English there, and getting picked up by drivers with whom we couldn't communicate would leave us feeling isolated, stupid, and apologetic without the means to apologize. We hadn't considered that not speaking the language would make it generally more difficult to live on our wits, and that living on our wits would be especially important given our meager supply of weak dollars.

A couple weeks into our trip, it became clear that it was going to be terrible. Not terrible and wonderful, as traveling in the States had often been, but pure, rotten badness. We got scabies in London. Carl kicked me in the stomach in Amsterdam. He punched me in the arm in Hamburg. He threw a can at me in Berlin, where I took to bed in the flat of the person we were crashing with, refusing to move or to talk for a day. Some of my greatest moments of shame come from considering the impression we must have made on those who housed us—friends of friends, mostly, along with a couple from Philly that we already knew. When the guy of that pair asked about the deep purple bruise on my shoulder, I told my lie in a flat voice: "I must have bumped into something." I recognized it as a standard line given by people who had been battered. But I wasn't one of them, was I?

WE WERE STILL having a lot of sex—scabies-scabbed bodies sawing into each other in strangers' living rooms, in strangers' barns, in tents pitched in small stands of woods—but it no longer cleared the air or relaxed me. The fucking became mechanical.

"Do you always want to have sex?" Carl asked me one day on the border between Germany and France, where the driver who had dropped us seemingly called forth every word he knew in English in order to tell us to watch out, that there were police and bad people here.

"Yes?" I said, unsure both of the truth and of the correct answer. "Do you?"

". . . No! Sometimes I'm just worried about getting you across the road and to somewhere safe and what are we going to eat and . . . no. Not always."

But we had sex that night in our tent in the weeds at the border, and we had sex the next day in a hotel room we sprung for in Strausbourg. Then I flooded the shower because I didn't understand its unfamiliar configuration, igniting another fight.

Spain started off a little better. It was sunny and warm, at least. I was so taken by Barcelona, I thought I could enjoy it despite our relationship's strain. But on our second day there we got into another screaming fight in front of the PicassoMuseum, where we dithered about spending the money to get in. Our fight wasn't about that, of course; it wasn't about anything. Or it was about everything—being poor, being languageless, being sick of each other. It was about Carl wearing a full set of long underwear under black jeans and a black wool sweater even though it was finally summer. Looking at him sweating, frowning, fussing, I couldn't stand it one more minute.

"We need a break from each other," I said to him. "Let's separate for the afternoon." He didn't want to, but I pressed on. Now our fight had a focus. I walked away from him, left the park, rounded a corner, but he followed me.

I turned, screamed, "I need a break! I need two hours by myself!"

Finally, he acceded.

"Give me the key to the room," he demanded. "Give me the money belt."

I did.

But I had in the pockets of my army surplus pants fat handfuls of gold pesetas worth about two dollars each. I managed to use my poor French at the pension to gain an extra key to our bare-bulbed room. Within moments, I emptied my pack of everything that belonged to him, and I tore out the section of the map that would guide me to the train station. I smiled politely when I handed back the key, then I ran out the door.

I had just enough money to buy a ticket to London. I crouched down between benches and hid until the train came, so afraid was I that Carl would search me out. It was a sixteen-hour journey and I had no cash, no credit card, no food. The train hadn't gone far from the station when I started to relax enough to feel hungry. It was dinnertime, and I hadn't eaten lunch.

My seatmate was opening foil packets, breaking the skin of an orange.

She said something to me, gesturing to her spread. Determining I didn't speak Spanish, she tried again: "Please. I share."

Her English was not great, and my Spanish nonexistent, but we became friends. She was a vegetarian, too. She could see I had a bold spirit, she said, and she did as well. It was certainly true that we looked more like each other than like the majority of young women I'd seen in Barcelona, who'd been mostly highly glossed, cinched, and heeled. We were make-up free, with long undone hair. We talked about that for a while, why we wore the shoes we did, other things to do with being female in the cultures where we came from. Eventually, I told her my situation.

"My name is Remedios," she told me. "I think someone tells me it means 'helping' in English."

She was the first of several women I met on my trip back to England who made it possible for me to get there, who aided me as I regained my sense of myself.

My escape from Carl, though dramatic, was not absolute. It didn't take him long to make his way back to Sheffield, and we ended up rejoining for a few days in Philadelphia. It was a depressing visit, though not because of any tension between us. That was gone, along with the passion. But the whole community around the house was in a fugue. They'd just gotten word that Joe had overdosed in San Francisco. He was dead.

I went back to Oberlin that fall so grateful to be a college girl, so grateful for my decent family and my college girlfriends with whom I was to share a house. I was lucky. It was enough to simply acknowledge this, I realized. I didn't have to renounce it. I was proud of my adventures, but I was very lucky to be where I was, and safe. The levels of other people's privilege seemed less important, and I ceased weighing the differences between my fellow students and me. The relationship between genders appeared less inherently antagonistic to me, too. I fell in love with the punkest rock boy on campus and found a source of sexual companionship that came without combat. Our attraction for each other was not born from resentment and did not hinder our affection, and the combination buoyed an often mute camaraderie. We were together for a long time, and I don't recall ever mentioning to him that I had been sexually abused. There seemed no reason to; during that period I wasn't interested in seeing myself in that light.

I CAN FIND no sign of Carl's existence on the Internet. I don't know where he is, but chances are good that he doesn't have a college degree, a reasonable job, a stable relationship, kids with whom he has a happy bond. Most people do not have that quartet of things. The family he came from certainly wasn't intact, secure, or nurturing. Neither was Toshi's. I'm so conscious that mine was, that my children's is. I still work on finding the balance between gratitude and exhumation, between acceptance and empathy, acknowledgment and fight.

TWO

ADULTHOOD

After graduating from Oberlin I moved to Chicago. My first years there were marked by itinerant work and travel, and I didn't live in one place long enough to fulfill a single lease. But by the summer I turned twenty-six, I was a little more rooted, settled into an apartment and holding a job that offered me vacation days. I requested a couple in order to take a trip to D.C. to stay with a college friend and see my father's cousin Rebecca, and then I walked down the street to a travel agency and bought an airline ticket. When that night I mentioned the trip in the litany of events from my day, my boyfriend Tom grew alarmed.

"But that's the weekend after my opening!" His gold brows pulled down sternly.

"I know. I was trying to fit it in between then and the Fourth, when prices go up."

"You can't go then. There's a big letdown after an opening," he said. "I'm going to be feeling really vulnerable. I'm going to need you around. How could you not see that?"

I squinted at him. Even with his explanation, I still didn't see it. His deep-set eyes were more fierce than pleading. It was after midnight, and I'd just clomped up the stairs of his six-flat minutes before. I'd been hanging out with friends at the bar around the corner, and I was all horny, beery cheer, slow to shift my mood to accommodate his sensitivity. We were sitting in the kitchen, the only living space in his apartment. The back two rooms he'd made into his studio. He'd been working there on one of his sculptures, and the smell of cut wood and acrylic mixed with that of old trash and stale smoke.

Tom's preoccupation with his art-making and computer programming was one of the things that drew me to him. We had regular weekend dates, but most often evenings would find me writing at home or going out with my friends before I headed to his place. It was only a bike ride away, and he always welcomed me, no matter the time or my condition. I got to have some one-on-one intimacy, an interesting sex life, and somewhere to go to salve my late-night restlessness without feeling too bound. Since freshman year in high school, I'd been a serial monogamist who nonetheless complained that relationships chafed me, and this current set-up, with its combination of independence and dependability, felt like what I had been looking for, especially since I had found my own creative groove, too, and was less at odds than I'd been in the past. When I'd wanted Tom to come to Mexico with me that spring, he'd turned me down because he needed the time to prepare for an installation that was still many weeks away, and—in my view of myself, at least—I had accepted that easily. I prided myself on not being needy. His neediness now was confusing, annoying.

But the different ways we spent our evenings often left our moods mismatched. And then there was our age difference. He was twelve years older—the same age as Toshi— which created another list of pros and cons in my assessment of the relationship. I liked the gravitas his extra years provided, the way the gray mixed in with his dark blond hair, the wisdom he'd gained about what it took to be an artist. And I liked that he had no desire to fit in with a bunch of twenty-somethings. He was content to let me party without him, wasn't waiting at the edges of the crowd frowning if I got too exuberant, as Carl and my most recent boyfriend had sometimes done. But I didn't like his condescension, which more and more often seemed like a weapon. And our expectations about how we should behave toward each other were often different.

"I told you I was going to see Leslie in June. You never mentioned anything about that weekend. How could I have seen it without you pointing it out to me?"

"I didn't think I'd have to mention it. I thought you'd be more sensitive." His tone was that of a disappointed teacher.

"You're saying I haven't been sensitive?" My confusion coalesced into anger. "For two months everything we've done or haven't done has been about this show. Everything's taken a back seat."

I lit a cigarette, let loose a stream of smoke that joined the cloud hanging below the high ceiling. I'd come over hoping to have sex; I could see the mattress on the floor in the adjoining room, its twist of white sheets and rumpled blankets beckoning. But that was not where we were headed tonight. The fight was just getting started, and we could go on for hours. Maybe we'd roll around together in the morning, which was when he preferred it anyway—another difference between us. I sighed.

THE NEXT DAY, he brought the issue up when we were post-coital, and in the softening we had one of those couple's moments where each assumes that the accord was due to the other having changed his or her view. When it turned out that neither of us had, the tension flared again. But my plans had already been made! But his loneliness! But my friend! But his sense of abandonment! Why couldn't we just do something nice the following weekend? Why couldn't I realize what it meant for him to put on this show, to stand in front of his work like that, after giving so much, and then have nothing to look forward to? We went back and forth for days.

Finally, I rescinded my vacation request at work and sheepishly called my friend to tell her I was changing my ticket. As I tried to explain why, I stumbled over my words. I still couldn't quite make it add up, couldn't quite swallow altering travel plans at the demand of a man. I had lost the argument because someone had to, but I hadn't changed my mind.

My friend was cool with it. And my cousin, when she heard, was glad; she'd have more time for me. My father had urged me to call her when he heard I was going to be in her town, and, awkwardly, I had. I'd only seen her a handful of times in my life. The thought of more hours with her did not seem to me like much of a consolation for my giving in to Tom.

TOM'S OPENING took place in a loft in an area that housed a growing number of alternative venues. It was a warm, early summer evening, and I remember what I wore: a short black taffeta slip topped with a sleeveless red silk blouse I had gotten at a Philadelphia thrift store the summer I met Carl. My legs were bare, and I wobbled on chunky platform heels. I painted my lips with the same bright red lipstick every day back then, but I blotted and reapplied it twice that night to acquire exceptional saturation for the occasion. My hair was cut very short. I'd never been the date of a showing artist before, and I wasn't sure what the role required, but an outfit I liked seemed the first line of defense.

My last few boyfriends had been indie-musician types, and what I was used to was being the accompanying girlfriend at rock shows. The shows had been such a defining aspect of my social life that when Tom and I had listened to his Van Morrison records one recent Sunday morning, it had provided gossip for the neighborhood. There'd been a group of people who couldn't believe that a staunch scenester like me was dating someone from whose porch mass-appeal hippie music was allowed to drift.

"I've never seen anyone change as much in a year," said the boyfriend I had left for Tom. He'd made the comment after I said no, I wasn't going to see one after another of the string of bands he listed off. I welcomed the sting of disapproval. My choice of Tom was in part a choice to move beyond the indie rock world and into something of my own. Girlfriending at an art event, while still girlfriending, seemed a step in this direction. It seemed more mature, somehow, which maybe just meant less fun. I had wanted to go see some of those bands my old boyfriend had named, especially in cases where I'd have once been on the guest list and waltzed in for free. But I was sacrificing that experience for something else, something like an apprenticeship: I saw similarities between the writing lifestyle I wanted for myself and the weird isolation and act-of-faith art-making that Tom engaged in. As I walked down the weedy street toward the gallery building, a former factory of some sort that housed several spaces, I was nervous for him. Who would come to his show? What reaction could satisfy, after all the build-up?

There wasn't a throng, but there were enough people circulating through the gallery to create the air of an event. I was proud for Tom. His art looked significant. I was impressed with the ingenuity that allowed him to create in a small studio space a body of work that could command a blank, high-ceilinged room double the size of his apartment, and even more so by his ability to stand by with dignity and observe the reactions to his ideas and labor. The show had a provocative theme, the condemnation of routine male circumcision, and people seemed to respond more energetically than they might have to work generated for purely aesthetic purposes.

I'D NEVER THOUGHT about circumcision as an issue before I met Tom, which was not long after I returned from an extended solo trip through Southeast Asia. I was bartending at a restaurant I used to work in to tide me over while I figured out my next steps, and he used to come in for dinner whenever he had a gig at one of the design studios popping up in the once-industrial area. I felt a jolt the first time I had to take his order. Not only were his looks arresting—blond ponytail, bronze cheekbones, dark eyes accented by crows feet—but his manner was both aloof and sex-charged. He often wore a black turtleneck, and he sat with the posture of a pianist while eating his soup and reading his book. When he finished his meal, he would sweep up the crumbs from his baguette with a combination of tenderness and disgust, dusting them onto his plate. Waiting on him with composure seemed like a test. How to be professional, neither gushing and obsequious nor hostilely resistant to his magnetism? I erred on the latter side at first, but he came in often enough and at odd enough hours—sometimes it was just me and him at the bar—that we got to know each other. We started to joke, to share the minutiae of our days. The titles of his books prompted us toward deeper conversations as well. Art. Psychology. Feminism. The difficulty of changing cultural norms.

"Yeah, it's really hard to make the mental shift," Tom acknowledged one day when I was talking about how tricky it could be for women to claim their independence even when conditions allowed it. "I've done some work around circumcision, and I've found the same thing."

I felt my brain clunk for a minute in an attempt to compute what he had said.

"What kind of work?" I asked to gain time.

"Routine medical circumcision is unnecessary, and there are some groups out there who are trying to stop it." He was straightforward and serious, the zinging wit we employed through much of our conversation at rest.

"That sounds really interesting." I mirrored his respectful tone.

I was impressed. It was easy to imagine that he'd been met with various responses when he brought up this topic, and I admired the bravery it took for him to mention it to me, a younger woman he was interested in. (Because he was interested in me, wasn't he? Or was he not? A great deal of my energy went into discerning this.) And I was intrigued. I liked the feeling of being exposed to something new and weird, invisible but omnipresent. As the weeks went by and we talked about the issue further, I got a sexy little zap every time the word *penis* passed between us or I felt it pushing up beneath words like *intact*, *foreskin*, *tip*, *sensitivity*. He brought in some literature for me, articles and fact sheets distributed by organizations dedicated to ending the practice in the United States, and I quickly agreed with their conclusions: there was no good reason to routinely circumcise. It should not be a default procedure at hospitals. I talked to my girlfriends about it, and they fell in line, too. If we ever had sons, we decided, we'd keep them intact.

I FOUND A DESK JOB, and at the going-away party the restaurant threw for me, Tom and I made a plan to hang out on the same side of a bar. Once we started sleeping together, he talked more to me about circumcision, about the personal woundedness he felt, about the depth of his anger that it had been done to him. These were things I'd never considered before, and I sensed my mind opening to new thoughts.

"That's interesting," I said again. "I've never heard even one other man talk about that."

"It's difficult," he said. "Men are trained to not look inside, so there's that. And no one wants to view himself as deficient, as mutilated. You want to think the way you are is fine, that whatever you're missing is no big deal."

He had used classified ads to find other men concerned about the issue, to start a support group. When he told me about it, he laughed.

"You get some pretty weird responses when you put an ad in the paper saying you want to meet with men who have feelings about circumcision."

But usually there wasn't a lot of humor about the issue. I could see how careful he had to be when he brought the matter out into the light, and the price he paid: He made himself vulnerable to being seen as a weirdo, forwent the comfort of blending in. To what extent was I willing to do that in my life?

One night at his apartment he got out some art he'd made about his penis. This sounds risible, I know. It was common among my friends, as well as in the larger culture, to make fun of dicks and the dick-obsessed. I could hear the derision: "Three-fourths of the entire artistic cannon is about guys and their cocks!"

But the pieces Tom showed me were smaller, more questioning and less technically masterful than the work of his I was used to seeing. I recognized in them the boldness and messiness that I picked up on in the work of women like Kim Gordon and Kathy Acker: cunt, pussy. The power of pussy. Why not, then, the sensitivity of penises, too? Why not, then, complicate the penis's standing as simply an instrument of ego and domination? I saw a dialogue between Tom's work and body-based feminist artwork, as well as between his work and heterosexual porn, that I could identify with. I considered anew the way gender rigidity can cause deformities on either side of the aisle. I loved the feeling of exploring bodies and desire and injustice and injury alongside someone male.

TOM'S INVESTIGATION of gender and sexuality and his unique stand on masculinity was hot to me, but it complicated our sex life—although this very complication was also at first a turn-on.

From early on, he was quick to challenge my performance in bed. This took me aback. The sparks were flying between us, and our connection was so young—how could he have arrived already at the conclusion that my skills were lacking? But the crux of my astonishment was this: I'd felt sure I was a good sexual partner. I'd been so confident on this point it'd put a swagger in my step.

Tom's challenge led to me ask myself why I'd presumed this. Well, my partners had given me every indication, for one thing! But I'd been in a string of relationships with very young men, a notoriously unpicky demographic when it came to getting laid—or so says conventional wisdom. When I thought about it, I could identify the qualities I'd demonstrated in most of my sexual relationships: I had little sexual shame, abundant hunger and enthusiasm, and the ability to have successive orgasms. My performance in bed had a lot to do with being responsive. I liked to offer up my body. But what Tom was calling me on was exactly that abdication. I was much less interested in figuring out what the other person needed, he said. In between the waves of hurt and defensiveness, I could see what he meant. I believed the other person was in charge of that.

"It's really common in women. They have a few off-the-rack tricks, but they're impersonal. They think just by bringing their body, it's enough." I'd argued a lot about porn over the years, especially early on in my career as a feminist, when I was confused by the feelings it elicited in me. But now Tom was turning the conversation about straight porn on its head. The objectification of women made women bad sex partners, he claimed. There was no celebration of the masculine body. (I don't recall where blow jobs and cum shots came into this discussion, but perhaps we were talking about soft porn and cultural images that modeled themselves after it.)

"I do like penises!" I exclaimed sincerely. And I really did. I liked the way they felt in my hand and made me feel. I did not squeal or slap the magazine shut when one was curled out, as I'd seen some of my friends do, a reaction I always found curious. "But we're not really used to seeing them."

A few days later, Tom presented me with a large, square image of a penis—uncircumcised of course, semi-hard, nestled in its bed of pubic hair. I put it on the refrigerator of my apartment. I liked the high contrast of the black and white, the softness of the pixilation, the promise. I liked the vulnerability. I liked its totemic power. And I had the experience I sometimes begrudged men with images of women: I could stare, and stare, and stare, and make this image my own, divorce it completely from the subjectivity of its owner. I forgot about its potential shock value until two men came into the apartment to check on the heaters. One of them recoiled, wouldn't speak, made quite a show of being disgusted. I thought he was smelling a noxious gas only detected to the trained nose. I must have looked confused.

"He doesn't like your photo," the other guy said, pointing his chin at it.

"Oh," I said. Normally I would be aflutter with apologies if someone was made the least bit uncomfortable in a room I was in, even one not my own. But I was reminded by this lunk-headed response how much I liked Tom's boldness. How proud I was of my own. I just shrugged.

BUT AS TIME went on and our personal relationship complicated, I grew to think Tom's interest in the issue of circumcision bordered on an obsession, that it went too far. He felt aggrieved, and I could not always maintain understanding. He was still angry with his parents for allowing it to be done to him. But surely, I ventured, they'd had only decent intent. Surely there was a point at which one had to just accept an irrevocable decision of the past, see it within its context. I counted myself a proponent of self-awareness, of questioning the status quo, of thinking things through. But Tom had examined this very closely, for years. Why keep poking a finger at the wound, when it couldn't be undone? Why not take satisfaction in the way he had channeled his hurt into helping change attitudes?

"You've already made a difference with me and my friends," I said. "And with a lot of other people, too. It's working. Like you said, the rates in the hospitals are going down. That's amazing."

"But it's a double-edged sword," he said. "The more that people realize it's wrong, the more people who will see a cut penis as a deformity. My advocacy is making me less desirable."

I saw the brutality of his point. But I also grew suspicious of him.

Statements like these made me wonder how much Tom's passion about circumcision was an effort to pull the mantle of victimhood into his own lap. I'd asked this of myself over the years, as well. Is that why I, a professor's daughter, carried a working-class chip on my shoulder? Is it why I harbored thoughts of my sexual abuse? To those of us who were liberally educated at a time when identity politics was informing the theories of just about everything, it was tempting to assert the legitimacy of our voices by accentuating the ways in which we'd been othered, been hurt by the hegemony or the powers that be. It could be frustrating to be categorized by race or gender as a member of an oppressive class when experiences in your own life left you feeling queered and marginalized. A sensitive white man must have felt this especially keenly.

But circumcision was an imperfect pivot point, because at the center of the movement away from it was a nice group of female nurses who sought to educate new parents about the repercussions. There was no categorically clear enemy, no neat flipping of accusation away from one gender and toward another. Certain segments of the men's rights groups that overlapped with the anti-circumcision groups seemed almost disappointed at this.

Tom was the first person I knew to discover the Mosaic Internet browser. When he'd begun his research on circumcision, he'd gone to libraries, posted classified ads, ordered pamphlets, and sent letters back and forth across the country. Now, every night he was able to connect instantly with new people and sources of information, which fueled his interest. On his computer and on pages he printed out for me, I looked at countless diagrams and pictures of penises—circumcised ones, uncircumcised ones, ones that had undergone botched circumcisions. I was fascinated at first, but eventually so much talk about foreskins and the descriptions of retraction, slip, glide, and ebb, became too much.

There was a shift in me, and I tipped toward aversion. I was reminded that Toshi was uncircumcised. It could be that I had never quite articulated that fact until I had access to so many images of penises. But now, as I read the literature, I started visualizing the head of the first one I'd seen push out of its foreskin as I held it in my hand.

Toshi had arrived at our house at the beginning of a school year, and at the end of it, he piled into the Ford Galaxy hard top with the rest of us and the family dog. We were all on our way to Albuquerque, New Mexico, where my father would be doing research for the summer. The days on the road had a rhythm. We ate breakfast and lunch from fixings my parents kept packed in a white Styrofoam cooler and flat-bottomed grocery bags. Breakfast was cereal in the plastic bowls my mom had brought from home, with milk poured from slim quarter-gallon cartons. Lunch was eaten around rest stop picnic tables: squished peanut butter and jelly sandwiches for my brother and me; for my parents, sardines and saltines. Toshi could go either way. We'd stop in the evening to eat dinner at a restaurant, something we seldom did at home. I felt a thrill of excitement and misgiving whenever we walked into one, having discovered that foods I thought I knew—chicken, noodles, even chocolate milk—could taste different in each new place. Then we'd check into a motel room with two double beds, and Toshi would sleep on a cot.

My mother still talks about the arduousness of the trip, the crowded conditions. Before we left, she had purchased for my brother and me a toy for each day of the road. But as a way of keeping us placated, it backfired. We'd start nagging for it as soon as we pulled out of the motel each morning. When she'd finally hand them out after lunch, either one would break immediately, or my brother or I would become fixated on what the other one had and start another loud battle. But I don't recall any misery, just the sleepy heat and crunchy grass of the rest stops and the force of will that drove us.

The house we rented in Albuquerque was fancy, at least relative to what we were used to. It was leagues away from the bare-bones four-room rental we'd spent the sabbatical year in two years earlier, and more spacious and luxurious than our cute little stone house at home. A one-story Spanish co-lonial, it was built around three sides of a courtyard that housed large terra cotta planters and a fish pond lined in blue and white tile. The fourth side of the courtyard was separated from the street with a high wall into which was cut an arched doorway closed off with a wrought iron gate. You had to walk through the courtyard to reach the front door, and so a mood was set before you entered the home. I remember being stunned the day we arrived. Outside the walls the sun shone mercilessly in the turquoise sky. Inside, there was shade, the gurgle of water, the cool of the tile and moss, the slip of the orange and white carp beneath the pond's murk.

The carved wooden door opened into an airy entryway lit with a sky-light and laid with red tile. There were three different directions you could step. I had just turned five, and how could I know this, but I would bet money that the structure was a traditional adobe, not plaster. The thick solidity of the walls was palpable immediately, even to me. Unlike our house at home, you couldn't hear what anyone else was doing in another room. Behind the house, in the backyard, things were less exotic but still very nice. There was a patio, a lawn, and a wooden swing set the likes of which I'd never seen. I made friends with children in the neighborhood, and we'd run back and forth between their house and ours, delighted by our quick bond and new freedom. I loved it. Being in Albuquerque made my mother noticeably happier, too. The summer had a shimmer.

BUT THE GREAT PRIVACY that the house afforded, along with days uninter-rupted by school, allowed Toshi to ratchet up his attentions. Instead of just coming to my room at night, he also began seeking me out during the day. The neighbor girls and I liked to play hide-and-seek, taking advantage of the deep closets and multiple hallways of our rental house. I was a good hider, and sometimes he was the only one who could find me.

I'd jump when I heard the whisper of denim or breath, thinking I had been caught. Then my reaction would shift. Not caught, but . . .

"Want to play?" he'd say.

"I am playing. Shush. I'm hiding." He'd come closer, crouched close to the floor, like I was. His hand would work its way into the leg of my shorts. I'd push it away, shift my body.

"Just a short one."

"Not now. I'm playing with my friends." I felt the difference between the airless space he created and the expansive thrill of fun he was keeping me from.

A bright light of clarity: Hide and seek was a game. He'd never been offering me a game.

He seemed to be there at every turn that summer. When I said no now, he did not listen. His hand reaching in. The unwanted burn and tingle. The extra tension during hide and seek knowing there were two parties looking for me. Or, at other times, that there wasn't anyone else who could see me, that he could get me alone more easily because the house was big.

Toshi and I were not in any accord in that house—not both toddlers, not both teenagers. We were each acting our new ages. A child wanting to play. A man wanting pussy. In the vocabulary available to me, I could finally articulate this much to myself about what was happening: Toshi was bugging me.

In comparison to him finding me in the daytime, my time, when there was real fun to be had, his coming to my bed would have almost been a relief. I had already ceded the night to him, to that. But he had started wanting other things from me at night. For me to touch his penis, his hand over mine, pulling the foreskin over the head, then away from it. The memory popped like a flash decades later when I read the word *slip* in Tom's circumcision literature.

"Now you try it." I didn't want to try it. My hands didn't want to hold as firmly as he insisted. His hands would cover mine again. "Harder. Like that."

And he wanted to put his mouth on my . . . what? The only words I had at the time were *down there. Under the underpants. Over the underpants.* I wore thick white cotton briefs dotted with blue flowers. He'd use his middle and index fingers to pull the fabric taut at my crotch, and he'd put his mouth just above it and blow as if trying to fog a window. The circle of his hot moist breath made me squirm. Then he'd gum the whole of my vulva.

"Does that feel better? Or does it feel better when I do this?"

"I don't know."

"What about this?" He'd move the fabric of the underpants aside and put his tongue in my cleft.

"It doesn't feel good."

"It's supposed to. Let me try it again. Like that?"

ONE DAY, my parents and brother were on an outing, so Toshi and I were entirely alone. I had stayed home because I was sick with a fever, bedridden. I was lying in a room I didn't usually sleep in, on a single bed in the middle of the tiled floor. There was one window located high on the wall. From a hook on the ceiling in front of it hung a spider plant, its leggy green vines outlined in gold from the afternoon sun. Even resting there by myself, my body felt alien to me, my limbs too achy to move, my discomfort too great to allow for true sleep despite my blurring exhaustion.

I was dozing fitfully when Toshi came in. For a moment I expected him to take my temperature and give me two more tablets of baby aspirin to dissolve on my tongue, as I'd heard my parents tell him to do. They'd clucked over me kindly all morning: Was I warm enough? Cool enough? Did I want them to hold the cup so I could take another sip of ginger ale? But Toshi did not look at or speak to me. He asked no question about my comfort before he removed the blanket I had tucked to my chin. I whimpered. The air hurt my skin. My understanding shifted, and the consciousness brought a flood of dismay, became a new ache: he was not going to take care of me, he was going to do things to me.

My body felt weighted down by sandbags, and my lips must have been sandbagged, too. Without asking me if he might, without even an attempt to coax me, he took my underwear all the way off. The pressure keeping me pressed to the bed intensified over my groin, fixed my hips in cement. I did calculations: there'd be nothing to stop this, no creak of a door or stir from my brother. He bent over me. I felt the awful squiggle of his tongue, the erasure of my mind, my body. I'd need patience. The ceiling was the same off-white as the walls.

It kept not ending. A moment's pause, relief, just meant a switch to something worse. The thick house's silence. He unzipped and let fall his heavy jeans. His purple and red dick was in my face. It poked out from a thatch of black hair. Then his body was over me. My torso had felt chilled without the blanket, especially when the space between my legs was hot, but now I was too sticky, too warm. The flutters of his unbuttoned shirt formed a tent over my head, his chest subsuming me, suffocating, the only thing I could see. His panting was the only thing I could hear. I felt a knocking at my crotch, the ball of energy that still hovered there even as my whole body was taken over. His dick was butting at my slit, though I know that only retrospectively.

Then the sonorous two-toned doorbell cut through: *ding-dong*.

He put my underwear on, he pulled the cover back over me. He pulled up his jeans, his big belt buckle thwacking. He left the room. I heard the door open—portal to the cool courtyard, the orange fish, the smooth pond, safety. I heard low voices. I thought I was saved.

But the front door closed, and—silence. Still silence. The bedroom door opened, and he was back. He took off my underwear again. And his jeans. His dick in my face. His dick at my crotch. I don't know what I did with it, what he did with it, what he guided me to do. I don't remember that. I remember the ceiling. I remember the feeling of my personhood vacating. I remember feeling gone.

I was still so little, but I didn't cry.

"Toshi didn't give me any aspirin," I told my mother.

"He didn't! Did he come in to check on you?"

"He came in, but he didn't check on me. He never gave me any aspirin or asked me how I felt."

"Oh, I'm sorry, sweetheart. We probably should have stayed home, but we had already canceled with them once."

She was always nice to me when I was sick.

I DIDN'T CRY either that same summer when I decided to swing by my feet from the pair of trapeze rings that hung from the swing set. I was in the backyard alone, and I remember hatching the plan for a new trick. I was at the age—as my daughter is now—when playgrounds come alive with new, gymnastic possibilities: hanging, swinging, looking at the world upside down. I didn't want to wait until someone could take me to play on some monkey bars. I could envision myself doing it here, now. I dragged a small patio table over to the swing set and climbed up on it so that I could reach the rings with my feet. I grabbed one ring and put a foot in, and then struggled to keep my balance as I grabbed the other ring. Got it! But I lifted my other foot without considering that there was nothing else to root me, and I went swinging off the table, knocking it down. I hung by one foot, the other one flailing, my hands unable to reach the ground. I swung like that for a moment and considered my options. I didn't have enough core strength to pull myself up to the chains. Even if I could figure a way to unhook my foot from the ring, the grass looked far away and the closest part of me to it was my face. The blood pounded loudly in my head.

"Help!" I finally called. "Heeeeeelp!"

My mother came. I knew she would.

"How'd you even do that?" she asked me, but she didn't yell. And later, "Were you scared?"

"No," I said. But I think I had been. Scared was a very quiet feeling for me.

M y kids, on the other hand, do not seem to have many quiet feelings, and they find crying to be a very natural mode of expression. As I write this, my oldest is eleven. He kept pretty quiet his first dozen hours out of the hatch—it'd been a long labor—but he started crying adamantly the night after he was born. In the maternity ward, he was the kid with the lungs heard from afar, whose cry made the other parents feel sympathy as well as an extra swell of gratitude for the peaceful little bundle nestled into their arms. Maybe they also felt a shiver of fear—there but for the grace of. . . And indeed, the screaming in the hospital was just the beginning.

For the first year of his life, my son wailed for many hours a day, and he had a full-bodied, ear-splitting, most passionate cry. He'd cry because he was hungry, but he'd be crying so much that it was hard for him to latch on to my breast. Once latched, he'd nurse voraciously, but he'd pause periodically to pull away and cry. He cried every single time he was in the car seat, and almost every time he was put in the stroller. He woke up crying in the night and he started the day off crying each morning. He cried when he pooped and he cried when he farted. Unfortunately, his brand of flailing, athletic crying caused him to poop and fart more than most. And, of course, he usually cried when we changed him.

Some readers probably have him diagnosed already: acid reflux, lactose intolerance. Plenty of readers probably have suggestions to give: Did I try giving up dairy? Did I eat broccoli or onions that day? Did I burp him long enough? Put him down early and often enough? Swaddle him? Swing him? Sling him? Show him who's boss? At some point I quit listening. I'd say what was wanted: oh no, oh yes, I did, I didn't, I tried, I'll try, but for the most part the exchanges just made me feel more despairing and alone.

In the evenings, my husband and I took turns holding him in the other room so the other of us could eat dinner out of the sight of the crying, a small relief, since his cries could still be heard. When Anthony had the baby, it took a force of my beaten, battered will to remain in the dining room. Part of me wanted to run far away, huddle in a cave of quiet or sidle up to a bar. But my greater impulse by far was to run toward my son and offer him what comfort I could as his heart-bleeding mama. You'd never believe it to hear him wail in my arms, but he actually cried less vehemently there than anywhere else. When he was not on me and I heard him in distress, my hands would twitch, my breasts would throb, my muscles would contract until my breath was forced into my throat. *Give me my baby!* Sometimes, even when he was quiet, or sleeping, or I was away, I'd hear a sound at the same pitch as his cry and I'd gasp and startle, alert. *Does he need me?*

The only thing that kept me seated, crouched on the chair like a gargoyle with both feet on the seat while he cried at dinnertime in the other room, was the search for knowledge to help him. As I shoveled food in my mouth, I paged frantically through the hodge-podge of baby books I had on hand. I was looking for clues, secrets, instructions, suggestions, comfort—albeit in a highly discombobulated and haphazard fashion. But mostly what I got was a series of admonishments from strangers certain they had the formula for all the tiny persons who came into the world. Some of the admonishments were cutesified, and some stern and science-based, but as the advice continued to crumble in my clumsy hands, all of it seemed to me smug and off-base. To describe my son as "fussy" was so understated as to be comical, and the authors who long-windedly explained that I do something as obvious as pick up my baby when he cried made me want to throw their books across the room.

Of course, there were also those who advised that I set my son down more—that the pick-your-baby-up theory was the root of much dysfunction. The single commonality among the books was their interest in scoring points against the other child-rearing schools. None of them acknowledged the depth, complexity, and individuality that I felt in my bones to be the pulsing heart of a human born to this earth, as well as that of a newly minted parent. All my life I'd felt allergic to self-help books, as well as to therapy and archetypal explanations, which I lumped all together. Though I tried to overcome my aversion when my baby was born screaming, the easiest thing for me to do when the books on hand didn't give me clear answers was to let my prejudice against so-called experts be confirmed. *Fuck you*, I started thinking about the books. *You don't know my baby. You don't know me.* I fell back on what I always had when it came time for me to move forward or into or away from something: the belief that I'd do better to figure it out for myself, to feel my own way, trust my own gut. Now I had the responsibility for someone else, too, yes, but I'd gather him up and offer my body and love while we muscled our way through.

Eventually, the pediatrician ventured a diagnosis of severe acid reflux, something that at the time doctors were just starting to understand better in infants. We ended up making a few visits to the gastrointestinal clinic, where tests were run and we were prescribed medicine. We also got a sense of perspective, as some of the parents and children in the children's hospital were clearly dealing with issues of greater long-term consequence than we were. In the clinic and labs, doctors, technicians, and other parents responded to our son's size and relative health, never mind that his strength was demonstrated in the violent way he recoiled his body from pain.

"How old is he?" one owl-eyed young father finally demanded as my baby writhed in my arms, arching his back, screaming. We'd been sitting in a waiting room together for the better part of an hour. He and his wife had been speaking to each other in a language I didn't recognize.

"Fifteen weeks," I said. Ropes of muscle stood out on my arms as I held my son while he bucked against me. My back ached.

"She is twenty weeks!" He pointed to his daughter, a listless little bird who appeared half the size of my son, her head tipped onto her mother's shoulder. "Look at him," he commanded his wife in English. "Look how strong!"

The other mother and I looked at each other, the river of fretful love we were each pouring into our babies spilling for a moment beyond its banks. The big, crying baby. The small, silent one. The worry, the worry. I think what we recognized in each other was an almost voluptuous fatalism. We blamed no one. We excused each other everything. We had each come to the point beyond advice. All we really believed in was our love.

WITH TIME and medication, the symptoms of the reflux abated, but our son still continued to cry loudly and often. My husband and I grew to accept that he was a person who responded particularly dramatically not only to pain and discomfort, but also to any kind of frustration, disappointment, or unwanted stimulus.

As the years went on, he continued to cry much more than most of his peers, and more passionately. At preschool, the teachers decided he should be one of the first kids to graduate to the older classroom, because he had met the key milestones before most of the others. "But you have to do something about his crying. This won't work in the four-year-old room," the teacher said.

"But what can I do?" I said. He was at the art table, trying to write his name. The stem of the first letter came out crooked, and, as if on cue, he began to cry. Not a whimper or a whine of petulant frustration, but a wail as full-throated and immediate as if someone had smashed a hammer onto his fingers.

I looked at the teacher, my eyebrows up and with my arms open: *tell me!*

She just sighed. She handed him a sheet of stickers and told him to choose one. In a few moments he collected himself enough to select a blue star.

I was not above offering this kind of distraction, but it wasn't a solution. I could feel that this was going to be one of those days with him, that at the next wobbly letter or bump on the elbow, the tears would come again. And I couldn't read her: Was she—was everyone—thinking there was something I could do, something I had done to encourage this?

Was there? Had I? The questions looped inside of me. I veered between self-consciousness and defiance. I still skimmed child-rearing books, but ever more defensively. I had witnessed from my son's first days his propensity to cry. Were questions posed just the right way or the offering of the right series of positive reinforcements really going to allay his birthright?

THROUGHOUT HIS ELEMENTARY years, he always cried more than was deemed age-appropriate. Attempts at tee-ball and soccer were unsuccessful. Each time the ball came at him—or didn't—he'd stand his ground and let loose a wail. His crying was a regular topic at every parent-teacher conference we had. When other parents were volunteering in his school, I'd often get a call or email from them letting me know my son had a meltdown. As if this were news. As if we should be prepared to meet him with a ramped-up sensitivity when he got home. But we'd become inured. We'd softened into the crying. Of course we tried to help him cope, to look at things differently, to take deep breaths. But we'd come to believe the best thing to do was mostly to accept the tears calmly—shrug it off and wait it out, as his friends seemed to do.

This is the point we had reached by third grade, when his concerned young teacher insisted he should see the social worker regularly. Whether due to the tips she offered him or some sense of growing social approbation, he began to turn his crying inward. His body would wrack as he tried to contain his response. He'd hyperventilate. For the first time ever, when tears overcame him, he would push me away. Crying caused him shame. He'd run up to his room and slam the door and cry and cry and cry. When he was getting ready to enter middle school, tears still leapt to his eyes at any hint of frustration or injustice, at any set back or splinter or sad thought or notion of struggle ahead.

Occasionally he cries in his sleep. If I hear, I'll go in to him.

"Shhh, it's just a dream," I'll say to him. I'll rub his back.

"It's just a dream?" he cries, his voice full of pained incredulity.

"Yes," I'll say. "It's not real."

He never remembers in the morning.

HIS LITTLE SISTER is still in preschool. When they play together, it ends in tears. The first ones might well be his. Then she'll join in. She's learned from the best.

There are seven years between my daughter and my son, in part because it took us so long to recover from the shock of our first foray into parenting. My husband and I were buoyant when we realized this new infant was not colicky. When she'd cry during the first few months, we'd look at each other, proud and disbelieving, and say, "*That's* her loud cry? That's nothing!" Whole days would go by without so much as a tear. A scrappy little whippet, with eyes bigger than her head, she could handle setbacks with aplomb. We have a video of her that I treasure, from when she was learning to crawl—so young, at just five months. She'd carefully lift one wobbly hand in front of the other and lean forward, and then she'd fall on her face. Splat. She'd pull herself up again with a look of blinky concentration and lift the next hand. Splat. Again and again, a dozen face plants calmly overcome until she reached my lap.

I felt so much relief. The whole world would seem a safer place to her. Her whole life would be so much easier. And parenting this one would be easier, too. She'd take after me, a legendary non-crier whose easy childhood disposition my parents still commend.

But I had to revise that theory. She came to her crying later, as a toddler. It was more an emotional and psychological rather than a physical response. While my son's crying rarely seems directed at my husband or me, hers almost always does. She seldom cries in school, the teachers say. She's amazingly calm. A very together little kid.

This kind of teacher report causes a different type of frustration than being told again and again that your child cries too much when you already know that as well as your own name. Talking to my daughter's teachers, I have the disconnected sense that I'm hearing about a stranger rather than my offspring. Because at home, for the past couple years or so, our daughter cries with incredible frequency. She cries if her socks are crinkled, because she wants to be carried down the stairs, because her stuffed animal has slipped in amidst the sheets. She cries because she wants some milk, some milk in the blue cup, not that much milk. She cries because she wants pants with pockets, because her shirt won't go on right, because I put her shirt on. One night she cried for half an hour because she surmised that George Washington—about whose dog we read a book— is dead. She cries if I look at her the wrong way, talk to her the wrong way, say words she doesn't want to hear.

She is physically brave and athletic, was quick to learn how to hang upside down off the monkey bars and to pump on the swing. She can fly herself high on the set in our backyard. But if she's not in the mood to pump that day, or if she wants me to look at her pumping and I'm not, or if an ant crawls across the slide, she cries.

Over the years I've learned the best thing to offer my son when he's crying is a neutral response and my presence for him to take or leave. I can do this, even if sometimes I must stifle (or try to) an impatient sigh. But my daughter's crying rattles me. It does what it's meant to. It pushes my buttons.

"Stop crying," I tell her. Yes, as accused by her, sometimes I say this in a mean way.

But sometimes I manage something better, in a patient and kind tone: "Stop crying and talk to me so I can understand what you need."

Sometimes I really have a good parenting moment and I get it, I can take the big view. "She's not really crying because she's trying to manipulate me into carrying her gangly four-year-old self while I lock the door," I remind myself. "She's crying because she's sad to say goodbye to me."

Then, after the door is locked, I can get down on my knees and say, "Is there anyone here who is crying because she's sad to be apart from her mom today?"

"Yes!" she'll say.

"Is there anyone who really wants a big hug?"

"Yes!"

And we'll hug for a long time, her little arms around my neck, the force of her love pushing me back on my heels, her pillowy cheek within reach of my hundred kisses. And then she'll start crying again.

All the crying in my house frays my nerves, leaves me spiked and sparking. *Toughen up,* I want to tell both my kids. Sometimes I do tell them. I'm a breathe-through-the-pain kind of person. Or shrug off the pain. Step away from it, analyze it. Box it up to look at later. Think of something else. Burrow into yourself and away from it. Run.

The very difficult thing for me about my emotional and talkative children is that they foreclose my use of some of these strategies. They're always knocking on my mind's door, or just barging in. Even when I insist on privacy, when I need it, they jangle the lock incessantly. I *can't* run. I can be thigh to thigh with my daughter, and she senses when I'm trying to find some peace, rise above, keep my patience by escaping the cacophony. "You're not really looking at me." "Why are you talking like that?" "Why are you making your eyes that way?" "Mama!"

I've gleaned from my half-hearted child-rearing research and from the factoids that float through the air of middle-class parenting ecosystems like so much cottonwood at allergy season that it's important for adults to respect kids' emotions so the children can learn to identify and respect their own emotions, too. Self-esteem and all that. But some days I wonder if there isn't such a thing as too much respect for emotions. The edict of paying very close attention to the hurts we feel contrasts with some other floating notions I encounter in my yoga classes, from my meditating friends, and during my occasional inquiries into Buddhism: feelings are just feelings. They come and go. They pass. *Shhhhhhh.* Let's quit talking. Let's lie on the grass and watch them gather and then disperse.

I try this out on my son. He's old enough to get it, and a positive side of his attuned sensitivity is that I can have some interesting conversations with him: "What if when you feel scared or sad, you just watch the feeling instead of crying about it. Maybe it will just pass."

He agrees it's worth a shot, but the next time he talks about a question he might have flubbed on a math test, his eyes well up, his face turns red. He cries.

I KNOW MY SON and his crying well by now. I'm getting to know my daughter's. But at heart their way of responding remains mysterious to me. What is the evolutionary function? Could there be a benefit to it? Might it in some way protect them?

My daughter is now the age that I was when Toshi moved in with us. I'm very conscious of this. It can awake in me a fierce protectiveness as well as a sense of woundedness when I wonder at her and how small I once was, too. Sometimes I listen to her prattle and contemplate how much she seems to live on the surface. By this I don't mean that she is superficial—she offers us the surprising nuggets common to thoughtful young children; she's clearly thinking about how the world works. But she is so willing to let family members see where her mind goes. Perhaps I appeared the same way to adults when I was her age, but my perception of myself is different. I remember wanting to keep my thoughts secret, to not let others, especially grown-ups, in. For example, when I played with puppets or dolls, I did so silently. I didn't want anyone listening to what I was imagining, so I conducted their conversations all in my head.

And, perhaps just once, I contrasted myself to my daughter in another way, too. She was crying for the fourth time that morning because, after she refused to put them on herself, I pulled up her underwear too quickly and my broken nail scratched her thigh. Frustrated at having to make elaborate apologies after tending to her all morning, I had this thought: *look what happened to me when I was four, and I never cried.*

WHAT MIGHT HAVE happened if I had cried?

ONE NIGHT I had a convoluted dream in which a young adult me was staying with some very young children in a compound owned by a family member who I knew to be a pedophile. I cried with relief when a maternal figure pulled me aside to tell me she had given the man some pills to kill his libido, because on my own I had not found a solution to the problem. I had not been able to take a bold action.

MAYBE I SHOULD be glad my children both cry so easily. It's difficult to conceive of my son suffering silently through anything that makes him uncomfortable, that makes his body feel not right. It's easy to imagine my daughter's stoicism outside the presence of close family, but it's hard to imagine she'd keep it together in my presence, where she'd probably screech through tears.

Yet I still have trouble seeing the advantages of crying. Here's where I've landed: if someone touches my children in a way that invades them, I don't want them to cry. I'd rather my son draw from his well of passionate umbrage, for my daughter to channel all of her demanding outrage, for them both to let loose a howl that shakes floorboards and windows, that draws the world's attention. Then I'd want them to breathe fire that would burn away any confusion, that would smote anyone who would impose his will on the body of a child.

At least that's what I wish I could have done. I still wish I could do it now.

After I'd agreed to postpone the visit to my friend in D.C., Tom drove me to the airport so that I could book a new flight. In an effort to move beyond all the fighting that had led to this errand, we were making a date of it. Tom had offered to pay the change fee and buy me some beers in the airport bar where we'd spent a fun evening awaiting a delayed flight of my mom's a month before.

As we approached the terminal, we walked past a family of Hasidic Jews. I liked the look of the men. Their flapping black jackets, their wide-rimmed fedoras, their long beards and sidelocks seemed both fashionably gothic and weirdly culturally specific to me, a dramatic reminder that I was living in a diverse big city, which still gave me a thrill. I turned to Tom to tell him so, but he offered his observation first.

"When I see them, it's like I'm looking at monsters."

"What?" I tensed. "Why?"

"Because they're responsible for circumcision," he said, as astonished by my question as I was by his statement.

I stopped walking. Tom took another step, then turned back to look at me while people pushed past us.

"But it's a religious ceremony for them. They're not responsible for routine hospital circumcision. For yours."

"They're the ones who've pushed it on everyone else."

"I don't think that's accurate. They don't even want to be like everyone else."

"The whole obsession with what's clean."

I shook my head, trying to reset the conversation. How could we even be debating this?

"You can't call them monsters because you don't agree with their religious practice. That's completely dehumanizing. That's anti-Semitic!"

"It's going to be hard to have a conversation about this if you're only going to respond with knee-jerk political correctness," Tom said.

So much for people-watching, for catching an easy beer buzz. We'd found the theme for our date.

MY DAD'S SIDE of the family is Jewish. I was raised celebrating Christmas without question and going to the Unitarian Church, and I was conscious of not being Jewish under Jewish law because my mother was a lapsed Catholic. But my mother was also an only child, without cousins, and whose own mother had died before I was born, and my Jewish relatives were the only extended family I knew. Every year we went to Pittsburgh to celebrate Passover with them. Back home, our taste for matzo and hamantashen and even bagels—only recently available in the local grocery stores' freezer sections when I was a kid—made us stand out in a town with just a handful of Jewish families. But we stood out in Pittsburgh for our goyish small-townishness, too, and for our ignorance of custom, even amidst the secularism. When it came to religion, not fitting in was the strongest part of my identity.

By late elementary school, I wanted to rectify this. I was craving clear answers to questions about what was true, about how to live and how to be good, and I started attending Sunday school and church with an elderly couple who lived nearby, around the wooded bend in a little house on a hillock. My mother drove me to their place each week, and I'd sit in the couch-like back seat of their sedan as they drove into town. Another friend's family had given me a white leather Bible, and I assigned myself readings from it, trying to get through two pages every night. At Sunday school, before we'd break out into age-specific classrooms, all the kids would sit in rows of cold, gray folding chairs for a lecture on the theme of the week that would be capped off with Bible drills.

The teacher would call out a verse: "Matthew 5:44!"

We'd pull our Bibles to our laps and flip through the onionskin pages. I was quick on the draw, my hand regularly darting up among the first.

"Zoe."

"Matthew 5:44. 'But I say unto you, love your enemies, bless them that curse you, do good to them that hate you, and pray for them which despitefully use you, and persecute you.' Matthew 5:44"

I felt so good when I won the drill and got to read the verse. I felt so virtuous when I put my coins in the collection plate at service. But after a year or so of this, my allegiance crumbled all at once when the lecture was about ascension into heaven. I raised my hand to ask what would happen to my cousins when they died, since they were Jewish and didn't believe in Jesus Christ.

"Unless they accept Christ as their savior, they're going to hell," the teacher said. I felt my face get hot.

"But they're good people," I replied.

"That doesn't matter. If you want them to go to heaven, you need to convince them to accept Jesus Christ as their savior before they die."

"But what about my father?" I blurted out.

"Does he believe in Jesus Christ as his savior?"

"He believes Jesus was a great person."

"He's got to believe that Jesus Christ is the son of God and his personal savior, or he's going to hell."

I stared at the open Bible in my lap with my ears ringing and my face burning. My father was the best person I knew—never less than honest, and a hundred times smarter than the Sunday school leader, a thousand times more genuinely helpful, a million times kinder. Even if he had to deliver bad news, he'd never make someone feel the way I felt now, especially in public. A god who was immune to those facts when it came time to let someone into heaven could not possibly exist. I refused to believe it. I walked out of church that day an atheist, and my radar was out for anti-Semitism.

BELIEVING I DETECTED this bias in Tom contributed to the feeling of unease I still carried about my decision to postpone my trip—had I been bullied into it? Part of what attracted me to him in the first place was how articulate he was, how skilled at using his large vocabulary and knowledge of psychology. When I met him, I'd been questioning some of my patterns in relationships, some of my very ways of being in the world, and I liked the fact that Tom wouldn't let me get away with anything, that he'd call me on my bullshit. But it was beginning to dawn on me that his ability to do this didn't mean he might not be full of bullshit himself, or worse. My friends were intimating as much. My roommate, with whom I was almost romantically close, was particularly defensive on my behalf, as well as possessive, and she threw barbed comments at Tom whenever she saw him. Then he'd throw her hostility up at me when we were alone. When my postponed trip finally came around, it was a relief to leave the whole situation behind.

LESLIE LIVED ALONE in a sunny yellow apartment in Dupont Circle and was leading a quiet life, throwing pots and taking the time to listen to herself while on a break from law school. We talked and strolled and shopped and read and lay in her living room drinking tea or beer and listening to the music she'd recently discovered: Ani DiFranco, Sarah McLachlan. It was cozy. On my last evening there, I was loath to leave the lounging, girlish comfort, but I knew I couldn't get out of seeing my dad's cousin. Her husband Fred was on his way to pick me up, and besides, I had told my dad that I'd make the visit.

Rebecca and my father were about fifteen years apart, but they had been close as kids; she had looked up to him as a big brother. As she grew into adulthood, she had come to visit our family a couple of times, and once, we visited her in D.C. The four of us slept in her studio apartment in Georgetown while she slept at Fred's, who she'd just started dating. Her bed was also her couch, covered in a sumptuous Indian tapestry, and she had ornamented bowls with tangles of dangly earrings in them, and the city lights glittered outside the one large window. It was the most glamorous place I had ever seen.

Now she lived in Potomac. She and Fred were both lawyers, and she in particular had done well, leaving the non-profit sector for a successful private practice. With each turn Fred took after he got off the expressway, the houses were set farther back from the curving streets, the landscaping a bit more lush. Fine sprays of mist rose up from underground sprinkler systems, watering artfully trimmed hedges and banks of lush flowers. I'd never lived anywhere like this or even close to it. I knew that I had the tools to pretend familiarity, and that in doing so I might get the flush of proximate success, but as always in such circumstances, I was conscious of the masquerade.

Walking in the front door, the first thing my eyes settled on were Robert Indiana's stacked letters in a framed poster above the fireplace: L-O V-E.

"I recognize that poster!" I said. It'd hung at my great-aunt and uncle's house.

"I know! Welcome! Don't you love it?" Rebecca came out of the kitchen wiping her hands on her apron, a trim version of her short, round mama. "Leah! Sarah! Susan! Come meet your cousin! I can't believe you've never seen them. We're just having spaghetti, I hope you don't mind."

School kids, NPR, the steaming pot on the stove and the colander in the sink—even among the affluence, this scenario I knew. It made me feel warm and lonely, near and far.

We settled down to the table, and we made some decent small talk: my new job as an editor, their jobs, the kids' school, the culture of suburban D.C. I felt proud of myself, adult. I was doing okay volleying the ball around the table, helping to make sure everyone got a turn at conversation, keeping it clean for the kids and expressing interest in their social studies projects. But small talk wasn't what Rebecca wanted to have. I could hear the impatience building in her voice. Before we were even done with our food, she came out with it: what she craved were details about my parents' divorce, initiated five years earlier, but apparently still news.

"Your mother never appreciated your father, did she? She was always so critical of him."

"Well, there are always two sides." I didn't want to join in a critique of my mother. All my life I'd heard my father commended by strangers, teachers, peers, family friends. I agreed with every accolade, but I'd also come to understand why my mother had gotten sick of it, especially when he received high praise for performing the same basic parenting duties she did every day.

"How did you feel about them separating? Were you upset?"

I wanted to talk about my own feelings even less than I wanted to explain my mother's. I tried to answer breezily, to make a safe or impervious statement and wrap a little distance around myself. But she was a lawyer. She kept coming back to the question, asking variations of it until I began to feel embattled and confused.

I HAD ANALYZED my parent's marriage with my friends, but even within our talky tribe the subject had not proved overly interesting. There was no strong attraction-repulsion; they did not seem to be playing symbolic roles for each other; they were not involved in an elaborate contest of wills; they did not use my brother and me as weapons or pawns. They were just very different people, and their fundamental incompatibility had long been evident to me. Already in college when they separated, eager to prove my independence, I viewed the divorce from afar. I thought it didn't have that much to do with me.

And for the first few years, really, it didn't. We continued to celebrate Christmas as a family, even when they both moved out of state. They each came to visit me regularly, and continued to mix well with my friends—my dad took us out to dinner and engaged in long conversations, my mom came out drinking with us and took the joint if it was passed to her. It wasn't until years afterward, when they each became more seriously involved with other people, that I felt an ache, a sense of true loss that eroded my foundational toughness. This was especially true with my father, who was more devoted to his new partner, and upon whom I was more dependent emotionally, because his love had always come so easily, without argument or strings. But lately I had come to feel that his ungrasping love and his wide belovedness made me expendable. It was a tender spot.

REBECCA'S QUERIES moved toward the direction of Lynne, my father's new partner. I liked her, I said. I didn't know her well. I could see she was a perfect fit for my dad. He'd made it clear that they were headed toward marriage.

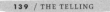

"Headed toward? They're getting married this Thanksgiving."

"What?"

"He didn't tell you?"

"No."

"Yeah, he told me last time I talked to him. You're going to go to the wedding, right?"

I managed only to shrug. I couldn't speak without revealing how hurt I was. Hearing this news from a third party confirmed my fears that my father's remarriage would alter my place in his life. I wanted to curl into a ball and hold myself as I absorbed the sting of the blow, but Rebecca kept probing for my reaction throughout dessert. When we finished our bowls of ice cream and strawberries, we moved to the den. At Rebecca's direction, Fred retrieved photo albums and boxes from another room, and I sat on the couch with a child on each side of me and one draped behind while the pictures were presented. Beneath the kids' squirming and climbing, the couch cushions moved so much there was the feeling of being on a boat. The family photographs sped through my hands.

"Oh look!" Rebecca said, pausing at one. "From Haruna's wedding! That was such a great weekend. Why weren't you there?"

"I don't know. Maybe I wasn't invited?"

"Of course you were invited! Everybody was invited. It's the last time we were all together. Here. Look. Look how beautiful Morris's girls are. I thought you liked them. Why didn't you come?"

"I don't know. Maybe I was out of the country. What year was it? I was traveling a lot around then."

"I think you just didn't want to go."

"Maybe I couldn't afford it. There were some years when I was really broke."

"Your father would have paid."

My father was indeed generous, but the certainty in Rebecca's voice belied a knowledge of how tightly the checkbook was balanced while my brother and I had both been in college. *You try living in our town with no extra money*, I thought, rising again to my mom's defense as I sunk into the luxurious couch in a house twice as big as the one I'd grown up in, on property worth ten times as much.

"Listen, I don't know why I wasn't there," I said. "I don't even remember anyone asking." It was true. I had no memory of the wedding, of a decision about whether or not to go. I glanced at the photograph. Haruna was indeed beautiful. All my life I'd thought of her as beautiful.

"Oh! The video of your father! Fred. Find that. Put that in. When they all came for Thanksgiving. Why didn't you come that year? Your brother was here."

"I might have been out of the country," I said.

"You weren't out of the country."

The VCR sucked up the video noisily. The TV came to life. Night had fallen by now, and the room, bare-windowed on three sides, echoed the darkness beyond. The screen was the fire, drawing our eyes, banishing the blackness.

THERE ARE NO HOME movies of me or my brother. We'd had no color TV until I was in high school, let alone a video camera, and I had disdain for the genre. But what I discovered in that den was that my unfamiliarity also meant I reacted to this footage of my family as if I were a member of a cargo cult, viewing something so miraculous that my confusion was transformed into awe. There was my father, his sister, her husband, my brother—all gathered at the house where I now sat, just as Rebecca said they'd been. The camera was focused on my dad, captured when his hair was less gray. He was pontificating gracefully, talking about early family memories, singing the praises of Rebecca's parents, his Aunt Yael and Uncle David.

"Yael was just this incredible person. She was so full of love, so full of life. She really brought the brothers back together. She was the cornerstone of this family. I felt closer to her than to my own mom and dad."

He was a beautiful speaker. My heart warmed to see him perform. His eyebrows were raised, his body relaxed, his pacing and breathing supporting the meaning of his words. He'd spent much of his career studying the oral tradition of Navajos, and I wondered which came first—his propensity for storytelling or his interest in a culture where it was fundamental. Watching him, I loved him very much. I wished he were with us now. I even wished I'd been there that Thanksgiving, and felt jealous of those who'd shared the room with him. A recurring question nagged me: Why hadn't he told these stories to me? Why had he devoted his career to documenting the lore of another culture, and, despite his general working-class pride, never shared his own family history with his children?

"The memories are not good," was how my father explained his silence about his own upbringing when I'd finally gotten around to asking. "For the most part, it was a very unhappy community." Once grown, he and his siblings all turned to other cultures to find a sense of meaning and belonging. And I had turned to subcultures and to my friends. Now he was getting married and he hadn't even told me. Had I become associated for him with memories that were not good?

The others' attention in the video waned. The photographs resumed their flow across my lap, the kids kept grabbing at them and swatting at each other, and Rebecca kept talking,.

"I'll tell you why I quit giving you things. Do you remember the last thing I gave you? That purse?"

"No."

"You don't? Really?"

"No. What purse?" My attention was tugged to my dad still flickering on the TV screen.

"When you guys visited us here, when you were little. You said you were going to move to D.C. Do you remember that? You fell in love with it. And I had this purse that you loved. With fringe. After you left, I sent it to you for a Hanukah present. And when I called and talked to your mother, she told me it was too nice for you to have and she kept it. You don't remember that?" She had stopped flipping through the photographs and turned to face me.

"That does sound like something my mother would do. I don't remember any of it though."

"You must have blocked it."

"Maybe. Or if I didn't know you sent it, I didn't even know to get upset."

"I got in a fight with your mother. I wanted you to have it. I sent it to you. How could she do that? You really don't remember?"

"Well, I was only what, eight?" A note of panic slipped into my voice. Here was a downside of the clan, of history and an extended family: the inability to leave anything behind, the power of others to decide what was important in your life.

"Rebecca, drop it," Fred said.

"And after that I never sent you anything, because I didn't want your mother to keep it. Oh, Look at this!" Rebecca interrupted herself. "It's my grandmother, your great-grandmother."

She showed me a sepia-toned photograph of a large and homely woman, framed by a disintegrating cardboard mat. The woman was wearing a black dress buttoned up to her chin. Her cheeks sagged like a hound's. Her eyes were all socket. "She had a nervous breakdown after her husband was killed, but they put her on a boat anyway with the kids, and when she got here she farmed them out. I think that's how it went. Or . . . you know you had a great-aunt that died when she was little, right? Maybe *that's* when she had the breakdown."

I didn't like this story, and I didn't like being related to a matron so mournful and lumpish, and apparently crazy to boot. I turned away from the photos spread out before me, from the home movie still playing, now showing just people's backs, the chatter and din of a table. There it was, the family clan, the place I came from, where love and meaning was supposed to reside, and it was so incidental to me—or I so incidental to it, rather. *Had* I been invited to these occasions? Or had I chosen not to come? Why would I have come, have left the drinking and dancing with friends for this?

And yet there was the undeniable blood tie. I felt the plasma coursing, channeled through something umbilical, muscular, looping and ropey. The knots of connection. And there was my mother, who'd once been a part, cut off from it now. Starved of nutrition, gasping. The image of her alone, family-less on the other side of a gulf, made me tense with a sense of responsibility. Even if I wanted to, I couldn't linger here. I needed to protect her.

"I'll make you a scan," Rebecca said. She took the photo from me when I'd held it too long. "You should have a picture of your great-grandmother. Fred, make her a copy. Oh, look. Here are the rest from Haruna's wedding. The ones with everybody. Well, everybody except Toshi." At his name I flinched. "He wasn't there. But he's always the outsider, isn't he? Just look at this picture. You can see it."

She handed me another photo. There was Haruna with her bleeding bouquet, a bloom on her cheek, her hair a black triangle, the ebony of Japan and the thick Ashkenazic curls from our fathers' side. Around the bride stood her stepmother in a kimono and her brothers and sisters, all tan skin and white smiles.

Fred came back to the room and gave me a copy of my great-grandmother's portrait.

"Thank you," I said, taking it, hating it.

"You can keep that one, too," Rebecca said about the wedding photo still in my hand. "So you have one with everybody."

"Come on kids," Fred said. "It's time for bed."

"Good night, you guys," I said. I was desperate at their leaving. As their energy dissipated, the black night pressed more tightly at the windows. I felt how far I was from my friend's place, how stranded I was in this suburb, this house.

I held the pictures politely. I felt brittle enough to crack.

"I always liked Toshi," Rebecca said. Alarms started going off inside my head. No one talked to me about Toshi. Why would they? Why was she? "Morris treated him so badly. It must have been disruptive when he came to live with you. What do you remember?"

"I remember Aunt Thelma and Uncle Jon and Aunt Carol talking about how Yoshiko was mean to him."

"But it must have been disruptive, wasn't it? What was it like? What did your mother think? Do you remember what your mother said?"

I was looking down at my hands. Perhaps I mumbled something. I couldn't hear my voice.

"I bet your mom didn't like it. I bet she gave your father a hard time. She gave him a hard time about everything. How did you feel about him coming? How did he treat you?"

My memories of this moment are all internal. Rebecca's questioning sent a violent shock through me. I was unable to recoil. Now, when I read the journal entry I wrote later that night, when I write what I think happened, I feel it again. It's hard for me to recall this moment without crying.

"Come on," she said. "You don't remember anything? You were old enough. What was it like? It must have been disruptive."

"Yes, it was disruptive," I said. I think I said it calmly, with the same distance with which I'd answered her other questions that night, trying to be cool to her heat, to send signals that I didn't want to say more. But the questions just kept coming—disruptive how? How did he interact with my brother and me? They weren't going to stop until I gave her what she wanted—because this was it, right? She knew, or she suspected. She could smell it on me.

Or not. Maybe she didn't know. She'd just said she always liked him. Confused, under stress, the only thing I could say was the bald truth.

"He molested me the whole time he was there."

Instantly I regretted speaking. I felt sick, hysterical, exposed. But my outburst had worked. It was quiet for a moment. I cannot remember the rest of the conversation. In my journal I wrote that we quickly switched topics.

As soon as Fred came back in the room I said I was tired and that I had to go. In the cushiony black silence of the car, I tried to patch myself back together, but I couldn't arrange my limbs to cover all my flayed open skin. I felt like a victim—less of Toshi than of Rebecca, that's on whom I placed my blame. I do not say this lightly: I felt like I was being driven home from a party at which I'd been sexually assaulted. Something elemental had been taken from me that I'd not wanted to give.

I walked in the door to Leslie's apartment.

"How was it?" She entered into the living room where I stood, a warm, golden space. She had a cup of tea in her hand. I felt a rush of gratitude for her, for her home, for my having of friends.

"Terrible," I said. I wilted onto the couch and started sobbing.

Every time I told someone I'd been sexually abused, I questioned why I did it, and many times when I thought about what my cousin had done to me, I wondered why I didn't tell anyone when the molestation was occurring. This second-guessing is common among both people who have been sexually abused and those who eventually find out about it, and the timing of telling or not telling is the cause of a lot of guilt and discomfort as well as some level of disbelief. As much as I haven't wanted to view my life as a single-issue case study, it's helped me to learn that there are common reasons why children tend to keep quiet about abuse, and that—although prompt disclosure can aid in kids getting the right kind of help—some of these reasons make a grim kind of sense.

Most children who are victims of sexual abuse know, depend on, like, and/or love the person who is abusing them. It can be difficult to recognize that a trusted person is doing something bad.

Once a child senses or recognizes that something bad is happening, she may feel implicated in her own acquiescence or confused or ashamed of the pleasure he takes from any part of the dynamic. The child may be reluctant to get an authority figure in trouble, or to call down dissent in their household or community. The child may doubt she will be taken seriously.

If it's a boy abused by another male, he may be afraid of being labeled as gay by a homophobic community, or worried about being seen as a potential abuser himself, due to the myth that abused boys usually go on to become child molesters.

It's likely that the perpetrator specifically admonished the victim not to tell, and may have made implicit or explicit threats about what could happen if she did, underlining what the victim already suspects or painting a vivid new picture: I'll hurt you, I'll get in trouble, you'll get in trouble, your mom will get mad, I won't be able to live here anymore, you won't be able to live here anymore, no one will believe you.

For these reasons as well as others, the vast majority of children delay disclosing abuse, especially when the abuse is ongoing.

Children who disclose abuse most often do so to a peer. If they tell an adult, it's most often a mother or mother figure. The response from that person can have a long-standing impact on the child, exacerbating or limiting the effects of the abuse itself. Experts advise that the listener stay calm and encourage the child to talk freely, that she assure the child that she is believed, that she is not at fault, and that she is loved.

But a mother may have a hard time accepting what she's hearing, especially if the perpetrator has been integral to the life of the family, providing money, shelter, safety, love. She may respond with horror, disbelief, denial, or hysteria. She may just sort of shrug it off, or retreat into depression.

Even if a mother responds in an ideal fashion—listening lovingly, getting medical attention for the child if needed, getting therapeutic help, which has been shown to mitigate the effect of the abuse on children—there can be dramatically negative unforeseen consequences when mothers try to protect their child from an abuser, especially when the abuser is the father. For example, mothers who accuse fathers of sexual abuse may lose some or all of their custody rights. Children who are taken in by their mother to report sexual abuse to the authorities may be removed from both parents and put into foster care.

The shift in the laws to acknowledge child sexual assault does not mean that the court system is easy on accusers. As with any sex crime, the justice system can have damaging consequences for the victims. Children who testify can be re-victimized by repeated or insensitive questions and by medical examination.

Despite research that shows that only a minute percentage of children give false testimony, there is still a commonly held belief that children can be manipulated and are highly suggestible in a courtroom setting. And with the damage that a charge of child sex assault can bring, the legal system must be cautious about handling accusations. Children can go through the stress of the trial preparation and trial and not be believed, be implicitly told that they're lying or that they don't understand their own experience.

Over twenty percent of children who report sexual abuse recant their accusations at some point. Research shows that most of the children who recant were originally telling the truth, and that family influences are what led them to rescind their testimony. They may be told that their family's troubles—emotional, financial—would diminish if the accusation went away. In many ways, these claims may be accurate.

We react with such visceral horror to the idea of children being sexual—let alone sexually abused—that it's easy to be incredulous about a victim or a victim's guardian doing anything but violently recoiling from the perpetrator and speaking out against him (or occasionally her) with confidence, certain that his behavior is the ultimate wrong. But from inside the experience, things can be much more complicated. It can be hard to get the words out, to get a ball rolling when its trajectory is unclear. There's no shame in that. Once you think about it, there's not even any surprise.

So it is the child who bears the burden not only of what was done to him or her, but also of what to do with the information about it, of how and when and whether or not to tell.

I told Leslie the story of the evening spent with Rebecca as best I could through my tears, including a brief version of what Toshi did to me. I went to bed spent but still mired, and I cried more in my sleep.

On the plane back to Chicago, I put the Ani DiFranco tape my friend had made me into my Walkman and listened to it as I looked out the window, tears streaming down my face. "I was eleven years old, he was as old as my dad, he took something from me I didn't even know I had," Ani sings in "Letter to a John."

He took something from me, I allowed myself to think. *But what? But what?*

When the tape ended, I pressed rewind.

don't ask me why i'm crying
i'm not going to tell you what's wrong
i'm just gonna sit on your lap
for five dollars a song
i want you to pay me for my beauty

i think it's only right
'cause i have been paying for it
all of my life

More tears salted the corners of my mouth.

TOM PICKED ME UP at the airport, charming and happy to see me. On the way to his place we compared notes about D.C., which he knew well. I was wearing a voluminous blue linen shirt I had gotten on my trip, and when we got back to his apartment I gave him a white one like it, and his face lifted in pleasure. He tried it on. I smiled at his smile as he looked in the mirror. Then he struck a pose, modeling for me.

"But are you okay?" he asked, seeing something quivering in my face.

"There was one part of my trip that was not very good," I said. "Remember I told you I was going to see my dad's cousin?" I started recounting the evening in a flat tone, trying to keep calm. But soon, I was sobbing.

I registered Tom's look of concern and compassion before he took me in his arms. His gesture staunched something, some embarrassment I was feeling about being out of control. I remember the billowing mesh of the soft linen, an enveloping. His reaction was a relief. I was allowed to cry about this. I was even getting something good through crying. He listened to me for hours, asked thoughtful questions about the dynamics between me and my parents, within my larger family. I talked about my confusion over Toshi. For the first time, I spoke about the abuse using more than the single sentence or two I'd always dropped previously. I noticed how each phrase nudged something in me, jostled me to let go of more. I let myself believe this was good.

THE NEXT DAY, I went back to my own apartment. I lived with my beloved roommate Monique in a small frame house divided into three units. We had the first floor rear; inside, the ceilings were low and the floors wildly uneven. The bedrooms were tiny and without doors, the better to let the heat circulate from the single space heater in the kitchen. All but two windows looked out onto brick walls. The house was near a busy street where prostitutes still strolled, and we regularly found evidence that they took clients underneath our porch.

But we loved that crooked little house. There were things about it that made it seem destined for us, the same way we felt about our friendship. The small rooms were arranged in such a way that if we forwent a dedicated living room, we could each have a room to sleep in and one to work in—a writing studio for me, a jewelry studio for Monique. Having a work-defined space was something important to us both, party girls distracted by sexual intrigue and romantic complications but increasingly pulled toward finding an identity based in our own endeavors. Not that we were done dressing up and going out. Miraculously, there were two walk-in closets, so the small rooms didn't preclude the storing of our costume-rich wardrobes. Getting ready for a special party or show, we'd blare PJ Harvey or Beck on the stereo and swap clothes, style each other. Mostly Monique would dress and style me. She could sew and bead, and had a bigger wardrobe and an endless stash of accessories.

She also had art and object collections and Turkish rugs, where I had almost nothing, and she decorated the place in a style that I aspired to. She embodied that style: tiny, eclectic, overtly sensual, worldly. She was half Vietnamese and had spent her childhood in France, and she adorned herself with a mix of foreign trinkets, repurposed thrift, and the occasional high-end piece bought by one or another of her former boyfriends. She made light, quick movements, and from her wafted the same scents that permeated the apartment: incense, smoke, whiskey, essential oils, and Aveda.

After Tom dropped me off, I dragged my suitcase along our dank walk-way, thumped it up the cement stairs of our porch, and turned the locks to our door. I walked the two steps it took to get from the entrance to our kitchen table and sank down. We kept the place cluttered but neat. The table was spread with one of Monique's fabrics and crowded with a tidy stack of my magazines and mail, and an iron-work bowl holding Monique's collection of oddly shaped light bulbs. There was the cylindrical marble ashtray we tipped our cigarettes into when we talked, but the lid was on it now, masking its purpose. There was also a note from her: "Welcome back, Goddess." Our schedules were different and we each had a boyfriend, and although we spent a lot of time together it was never clear when we'd next cross paths in the house. I ached for her, unsure what to do with myself here alone in the flat afternoon.

I went into my writing room to type into my journal. I'd kept one since fifth grade, but in that year between getting a computer and hooking it up to the Internet I documented my emotional terrain exceptionally thoroughly. Already that summer I had typed dozens of single-spaced pages analyzing my relationship with Tom. I had written many others analyzing my role in my nuclear family, the shifting sands between me and my dad. But never in any of the scores of volumes I had filled in my life had I ever written about Toshi.

"And then I go to D.C. and get perspective on this whole boyfriend thing by meeting my truly deepest pain and anger and need and loneliness and frustration," I began my newest entry. I recounted the evening at Rebecca's blow by blow, my fingers quick and strong at the keyboard, five pages turning into six, then seven. My typing stopped when I tried to address my feelings about what happened with Toshi. My wrists sank down and my fingers curled towards them. "I really don't like writing about this, do I?" I finally wrote. I stopped again. When I heard the jangle of keys at the door, I sprang up.

"Are you home, my darling?" Monique called out.

"I'm home!" I cried.

THE TABLE WITH both of us at it came alive. There was the bourbon, the cigarettes, the burrito from the corner place that she brought home and we shared. I told her the story. I saw her jaw set when I came to Toshi, a look of fire in her eye.

"Did anything like that happen to you?" I ventured.

"No," she said. "But I know it happens to a lot of people. And when we first came back to the States and we were staying in our cousin's house in Kansas . . . No, not like that. But I understand."

"Let me run you a bath," she said later. She sometimes pampered me, an exotic experience, as I did not seek out this kind of grooming. I had never had a professional manicure, did not own bathing salts or delight in creams or wear my hair in styles that required assistance. Allowing myself to be taken care of was a new frontier. But she had worked at department-store make up counters as well as in herb shops and in upscale salons. There was a whole cabinet in our bathroom devoted to her perfumes and potions. Pampering others was one of her skills, a way she'd earned money and a way she showed love. She lit candles in the bathroom and washed my back and then left me alone for a while. When I got out, I put on a silk robe I had previously commandeered from her rack of them and that had become mine.

"Let me rub your back," she said. I slipped the robe off my shoulders and lay on her bed, a proper one, not a futon.

She was so petite. Often in laying my naked self out for a man, who was always larger, I felt an invincibility. Perhaps it was bravado, an if-you-give-it-they-can't-take-it attitude, an armor I put on. Perhaps it was just the freedom of having made a decision, and the headlong leap toward thrill. I didn't feel that imperviousness with Monique. Laying still for her, letting myself be tended to girlishly, letting myself be big, I became vulnerable. I could afford to be. I always felt defended by Monique, and I defended her. We were a pair united not by blood or by any of the expectations or conventions of romantic coupledom, but by choice and provision. Our bond was entirely of the moment.

The tension I had held onto finally ebbed as she stroked me. I started to cry again, a release but not quite. My crying was a switch of roles for us, as she was the one to whom tears came easily, gracefully. She could have a conversation with them rolling gently down her face, and they weren't accompanied by rivers of snot and gasps for breath, the way crying usually was for me. I had done so much of it in the past two days that I was a little calmer about it now. My back shook and I needed some tissue, but I did not wail. Eventually, Monique curled around my back, and we fell asleep together.

OVER THE COURSE of the next week I sought out all my close friends. I talked and cried about my father and Rebecca and Toshi until I was bored, until I couldn't stand to talk about it any more. The knots with my father could be explained, traced, easily analyzed. The story had common touchstones—everyone knew of distant dads, divorce, Electra. It made sense. But my violent response to Rebecca's questioning about Toshi did not. I had long since come to terms with being molested, I told my friends. Given the particulars of my situation, it was just not such a big deal. I trotted out my litany: There was no violence. No physical pain. Toshi was a black sheep cousin, not my teacher or father or grandfather. I'd experienced no long-term ill effects.

But as I continued to find myself crying as I rode my bike home from work, or treaded on the Stairmaster, or wrote in my journal, I started to think the story was missing something. I began to mistrust my own analysis, my own essentially cheerful personality and functionality. Perhaps some psychological damage *had* been done. If I had near-forgotten about my molestation for stretches of my life, perhaps it was not because it was mostly incidental.

When Rebecca had used the word *blocked* to explain why I didn't remember a purse of hers I had liked as a child, I had scoffed at the way she was trivializing events worth repressing in order to explain away a truth inconvenient to her own story. But the term rang in my head. Perhaps I was responding so violently now because I had blocked a trauma, and didn't know what to do with my memories.

I t was 1994, and the term *blocked* had been common parlance for some time—Rebecca's use of it had almost seemed retro to me. Throughout the 1980s, childhood sexual abuse was a hot topic. The formerly taboo subject permeated the media environment to the extent that as a teenager I became aware of the related issues just by skimming through *Newsweek* and the *New York Times* and overhearing bits of news and adult conversations. At the extreme end of the discussion were the accusations of ritual satanic abuse, where whole communities of children were coming forward with stories about the sadistic treatment they received at the hands of respected community members, but there were also stories of individual abuse and incest, and new studies about the rate of such occurrences. Once I went to college, my sources of information expanded from mainstream media to include my women's studies readings, which were concerned with victim's rights and helping girls and women say no and to protect themselves. But whether the discussion was taking place in a cover story about cults in Montana or in *Our Bodies, Ourselves*, memories of childhood sexual abuse were often described as having been repressed.

Since before puberty, any discussion of sex caught my attention, and I was particularly attuned to stories that involved sexual activity and children. If I was looking for clues to help me understand what had happened to me when I was little, I did not find them. Quite the opposite. I read accounts of girls who were raped by their fathers or stepfathers; or who were tortured and sodomized—along with male children—by groups of trusted elders, and I could never square my own creepy but quiet memories with these abject horrors. And while many of the victims I read about had not been able to face that such atrocious things had happened until they were adults, I had always had a deck of early childhood sex memories tucked in my pocket, at the ready.

Upon my return from D.C., I studied the lists of symptoms of survivors in *The Courage to Heal*, reading it for the first time though it had been the best-known book in the sexual abuse recovery canon for years. I found few characteristics I could definitively claim—I did not feel powerless, I did not feel like if people knew me they'd leave me, I did not feel unable to protect myself in dangerous situations, I didn't feel conflicted about enjoying sex, or have trouble saying no to sex I didn't want, or engage in sex that repeated aspects of my abuse. I was fine. Was that another piece of evidence suggesting that what I experienced didn't rate? I didn't quite believe that, but I wasn't eager to be associated with a victim's movement, either.

Even in the eighties when childhood sexual abuse was receiving so much attention, there were those who doubted that the epidemic existed, as well as those who subscribed to the dictum "least said, soonest mended" when it came to airing uncomfortable family secrets. By the 1990s, the chorus of skeptics had grown. In particular, the veracity of recovered memory was challenged more and more loudly. One did not have to be paying any particular attention to the topic to glean this. Uncharacteristically, I did not cast my lot with one side or the other. In truth, although I pontificated snottily on any number of topics, I was not well informed about much. I relied on signifiers to direct my opinionated rants. Was something feminist? Pro-sex? Anti-Reagan or Bush or their ilk? Punk-rock? Then I was for it, and I had a grab bag of arguments I could adapt to fit the screed. Was it reactive? Militaristic? Hegemonic? Patriarchal? Then I was against it, for pro forma reasons.

I could debate whether to tack toward idealism or pragmatism on various issues, but this didn't make me fundamentally question where I myself stood.

But the conversation about sex abuse sloshed sloppily between the poles. Men using girls sexually, society not listening to women and children, religious leaders cautioning against rocking the family boat with accusations—well, all that is to be expected in a patriarchy, and it was bad.

On the other hand: Satanic abuse? That sounded like something a crazy holy-roller would dream up. And pushy therapists, experts, telling a vulnerable woman that they knew more about her life and feelings than she did, especially if they could monetize her need for their truth? That was The Man all over, even if the therapist was a woman. And it was no good.

Both being silenced and denied, and being manipulated and tricked, interpreted—just the word made my skin crawl—hit a deep, raw nerve. I would have preferred to look away from debates about the impact of early childhood experience, but my own recent upheaval was making that hard to do, and so were my friends. Even as certain parts of the psychological community were coming under attack in the media, psychology was increasingly relevant among the people I was hanging out with during the period in which I took my trip to D.C. Much of Tom's work and thinking were predicated on assumptions about archetypes and the formative nature of childhood. And for the first time, I knew of multiple friends who were in therapy. Jargon started to appear more frequently in conversation: terms such as *passive-aggressive* and *co-dependent* were thrown around knowingly, and I was embarrassed I didn't understand their definitions and kept forgetting after being told. Not being up on the lingo left me operating as if in a foreign country, and I missed the gist of some important barroom conversations. Alone, though, my friends did not use shorthand as breezily. They were eager to talk in depth about what they were discovering with their therapists, to share the interpretations of their lives and themselves that they were drafting with the help of a professional and the books she suggested, to offer me possible interpretations of my own life. I was both interested in and suspicious about their therapeutic insight. It occurred to me that they were jotting themselves into outlines as pat as some of my own lecture points were beginning to seem to me.

A: The Mother

    1. She acted like _____

    2. In response I formed a pattern of _____

B: The Father

    1. He was always/never _____

    2. So I tried too hard to be _____

Wasn't all the focus on family dynamics in childhood mechanistic? And weren't the expectations therapy seemed to have for parents just too high? In some cases I knew my friends' parents as generous and well-meaning, and I felt protective of them. If so many subtle shades of maternal attitude and behavior could knock a personality out of whack, I didn't see what hope any of us had, or how the species had produced anything of value.

In my own family history, I was conscious of the relative newness of middle-class expectations. It'd only been in the past generation or two that anyone related to me by blood had ascended the hierarchy of needs to the level at which understanding the effect of one's upbringing might be viewed as an imperative. Fresh from my travels in Asia, I was aware of how different life could look elsewhere. How the roles of mother and father and daughter and family were universal but hugely varied. How survival demanded different tactics in different circumstances. It seemed to me that where and when we were born had to affect us at least as much as who raised us, to say nothing of DNA. There was not a simple list of ingredients from which adult happiness could be baked. I wanted a wider view.

AND YET . . . I found myself crying spontaneously over memories of being touched sexually when I was a child. I was crying over my father remarrying and my mother being scorned and alone. This was such classic psychological territory. If I was ever going to try psychotherapy, now was the time.

One friend gave me her therapist's number. Another, thinking it better if we didn't share this, asked hers for recommendations for me. Tom had heard of someone who was particularly good at the mind-body connection.

"How much does it cost?" I asked my friends.

"Sixty dollars an hour."

"Does your insurance pay?"

"They pay thirty percent of the first eight sessions."

"But how will I know if I like them?"

"The first time you go it should be more like you're interviewing them."

"Do you have to pay for that?"

"Sometimes they'll let you have the first session free."

"How much does yours charge?"

AROUND THIS TIME in my life, I'd again found myself with a number of friends and acquaintances who were taking up various kinds of sex work. In Philly, most of the women I'd known who were stripping and prostituting weren't enrolled in college or emerging from solid middle-class backgrounds, but this time, my friends dabbling in the industry tended to be grad students whose parents had their own advanced degrees. They were smart, high-achieving women whose choice of part-time job reflected a rational assessment of the time-money factors as well as political and intellectual considerations shaped by gender studies texts. They'd read Judith Butler's *Performing Gender*, and they thought they might as well explore first-hand how the construction of femininity intersected with capitalism.

A year or so before I started dating Tom, feeling confident about my sexuality and trying to grow my bank account to afford some travel, I came closer than I had in college to considering this choice myself. Chicago didn't have a red-light culture that was as obvious as Philadelphia's, where a girl looking for a job could just wander into a bar she passed on her daily rounds, but to a pair of open eyes, opportunities to get paid for shucking your clothes still seemed ubiquitous. One day I answered a classified ad. A dare to myself: just take this one step. Adrenaline surged at each ring of the phone, exploded when a man finally picked up. The tone of his greeting alone, which as much as smelled of cigar smoke, started to close the half-open question of whether I'd ever try this. But I carried on.

"I'm calling about the ad for dancers," I said.

"Well, first of all, are you over eighteen?"

"Yes."

"You'll need ID. Here's how we do it. You can come in any Monday night, which is amateur night, from seven to nine. You come in, you sign up, you tell us you're looking for a job."

"Okay."

"Give it your best shot when your number is called. You win or you get runner-up, we talk to you about bringing you on."

The movie of this scenario played in my mind. A smoky nightclub, the dark cut by stripes of purple light. The voice of a jaded game show host introducing the next girl. Me. I pictured myself rising from my seat. Just this fifteen-second mental clip made my jaw set, my eyebrows furrow. I was expected to do this for free? At the intersection of constructed femininity and capitalism were girls getting screwed. That door slammed shut.

I FELT MUCH the same when I called the few therapists I did.

"I'm considering therapy, and you were recommended to me by so-and-so." But I'd spend the entire few minutes of our exchange wondering when I should ask whether I'd be charged for the first session, then bristling at whatever answer was given. Discussing payment felt as sexy-dirty, inevitable, and ill-fitting as asking about stripping auditions.

As I was making these calls, an out-of-town friend—one of those working in a strip club and to whom I'd written about my recent preoccupations—emailed me to warn me off therapy. "Proceed with caution," she said. I felt relieved to have my concerns validated.

When I was twenty-six, I was not yet ready to offer my memories and interpretations into the marketplace. In other words, it was my cheapness and anxiety about money that kept me away from therapy during a vulnerable time in my life.

If I was a rich girl and could shop for a really wonderful therapist, of course I'd go, I told myself. Of course not going didn't speak to any deeper fears.

MEANWHILE, I CONTINUED to peruse the self-help and psychology sections of bookstores, where again I made a connection to sex work, noting that in those stacks I felt akin to how I did in a porn aisle. Just being in proximity to the material made me hot, bothered, and embarrassed. Each book I pulled down and cracked open made me feel sexily, sickly bold. But there was one difference when the content was meant to inspire recovery rather than arousal: as I biked home, instead of rocking on my seat to get off, I might well start to cry.

This was getting old. If I wasn't going to take the therapeutic course of action, I had to take some other one.

THE ENVY OF OTHERS

G rowing up, I knew my parents were widely considered to be great. I mostly agreed. They were fun, enthusiastic, involved, parental yet permissive. Other houses had dads you had to tiptoe around if you ever saw them at all, mothers with perpetual headaches or long lists of don'ts, but not mine. They limited our intake of sugar, TV, and material objects, but when it came to activities, they allowed much. We could cover the refrigerator with Play-Doh creations, run wild through the woods, colonize the entire house with our set-ups and forts. Troops of friends tromped in and out. We lived out of the way, and it took a while to drive anywhere, but as we grew older, our parents let us attend any sleepover, sign up for any sport, or take any kind of classes we had a mind to. My dad coached, my mom organized and PTA'd and brought home boxes of books to feed my reading habit. Both of them did more than their share of carpooling, opening possibilities for kids who otherwise might have been stuck at home.

My dad, especially, was almost famous in our town for being a good guy. His likeness was included on a wall mural at a community center where he'd done some volunteering. Teachers got visibly excited when he chaperoned a field trip. And whenever we'd run into one of his students—especially the long-shot kids he made a point of mentoring—they'd tell my brother and me how lucky we were to have such a special dad. Sometimes they said it with an almost scary intensity. Even as I became more independent and was seen less often with my family, such comments kept coming. When I was in high school and working at a diner in town, several customers approached me to share some consideration or kindness of his that they'd never forgotten.

"Thank you for telling me," I'd say. "He's a great dad." I was proud of him, and I knew people looked at me with more interest because of how he interacted with the world.

In part, my parents stood out because we lived in a close-knit, rural, blue-collar town where many people weren't used to looking for social or enrichment opportunities beyond a family circle. But my mom and dad became known as the fun parents among the spread-out Zolbrod clan, too.

Toshi was the only Japanese cousin I met in the flesh for many years. The rest of them were figures in my imagination, spun largely from the exotic package we'd receive from them at Christmastime bearing foreign stamps. Some of their gifts are among my all-time favorites: a gold cat pin with a jade belly, a red tower-shaped jewelry box that opened with a pull of silk tassels, my own kimono. Each year, I'd study the family photo that came with the card. "Who's that? And who's that?" I'd ask my dad. The list of Japanese names played like music. So many of them—four kids—and all with such midnight hair, the color I coveted.

My eyes always settled on Haruna. She was the big girl in the picture, and then the budding adolescent. The category of teenager was for me synonymous with beauty, and the image of Haruna did nothing to complicate this view. In fact, it might have formed it. She was the movie star of my early life.

Finally, some years after Toshi had left our home, my uncle called to say he was bringing the whole family East for a visit. I had built them up in my mind to a height that seemed destined for a knock-down, but the reality of actual playmates was even better than the fantasy, and in person Haruna was not only beautiful, but—what bounty—friendly and willing to play with little kids. First we went to Pittsburgh for a visit, and then they came to our town. The six of us burst open our small house with our exuberance, turned every room into a stage for athletic contest and make-believe, raided my parents' closets for dress-up, thundered up and down the stairs, in and out of doors. My parents just laughed, as happy as we were. My mom took pictures of us all standing in the front yard, draped in layers of her clothes.

I knew their house was much stricter. Even in the midst of our heedless playing, I could see that my uncle held his body tight as he watched us, that he never laughed outright. I'd heard tales of the demanding regimen he enforced, of his authoritarianism and rigidity. A few years after the visit, when Haruna got to be sixteen or so, the same age as Toshi had been when he came to us, she started rebelling, too. Like her brother, she tried to run away. When her parents told her she was being sent to Pennsylvania, she agreed readily. She said she wanted to go to our house. They let her believe that's where she was going.

But when she arrived at the Pittsburgh airport, she was met by my grandfather and Aunt Carol, a woman of my grandparents' generation who had been boarding in their basement for decades and had attained nominal family status.

"When am I going to Aunt and Uncle's?" Haruna asked.

I was listening on the upstairs phone when Aunt Carol described to my parents Haruna's reaction to the bait and switch: she looked like she'd been hit. She'd been crying every night. She refused to sleep in one of the two vacant bedrooms on the second floor, and instead pulled down the ladder to my late grandmother's sewing room, a hot little garret still fuzzy with bits of thread, and stayed up there. Despite the remove at which she'd tried to set herself, her sobs wracked the house.

My family moved up our scheduled visit to Pittsburgh to help ease the stress on everyone, and I anxiously anticipated the trip. About nine years old at this time, I was developing a sense of self-consciousness and cool, even as I still played make-believe games and tended my dolls. My romance with Haruna had never ended, but it had taken a different form: she was less icon than model. I desperately wanted to rub shoulders with teenagerhood, and I developed a fantasy as I waited to see her: my beautiful cousin, now a sort of princess trapped in a tower, would recognize that I was older than my status as child implied, and instead of stooping to play with me as she had in the past, she would raise me up and make me a confidante. In my daydreams, my role was an amalgamation of peer and gallant savior. She would tell me all her teenaged sins, the ones my mother wouldn't divulge, and I would help to free her. We'd ride off together in a tinkle of dangly earrings.

The first moments in my grandparents' house shook me out of my fictive trance. Before Haruna had even come down from her room, my aunt produced Pittsburgh Pirates visors for my brother and me to wear to the game she'd gotten us tickets for that night. The visors were hideous. Something was off about their shape. Tears sprang into my eyes as I caught a glimpse of myself in the glass of the antique doll case. Standing next to my little brother, who was topped off with an identical mustard-yellow monstrosity, doubled the damage. Tweedle Dee and Tweedle Dum.

I feared Haruna would never be able to recognize the cool compatriot in me now, but I also was old enough to know that my Aunt Carol had gone to lengths to please us, as she always did, and that I had to be courteous. Not only did I have to say thank you, I had to act like I meant it. I had to keep the hat on. My instinct to do the opposite was so strong I felt my muscles flex with the effort of restraint as Haruna came tapping down the stairs.

"Hello Uncle! Hello Aunt! Hello Zoe and Julius!" Even her voice was pretty.

I'd decided that the most grown-up thing about me was my hair, finally truly long and with the bangs grown out. I had planned to greet Haruna by giving it a toss over my shoulder, but instead it was bunched under the elastic strap of the hat, poofing out from my skull. I felt like a grotesquerie.

But somehow my incipient teenager's heart could be seen, because that night Haruna invited me to sleep with her on the floor of my grandmother's sewing room. And so it happened, as I had dreamed. Over the next couple days, daylight saw us making strained family conversation, and Haruna barely talked. But when dark fell, she and I would climb the attic stairs and pull them up behind us into the muggy room, and she'd whisper her post-pubescent confessions to me for what felt like hours.

There was much I didn't understand, partly because she was talking to herself, really, with no attempt to fill me in on any background details, and partly because she was alluding to things between teenaged boys and girls and between teenaged girls and their parents about which I had only foggy notions. But I was wise enough to appear knowing, to nod seriously and meet her eyes.

In the hot space between her stories of embattled romance and my silence, a self-imperative grew: ask her about Toshi. Ask her about whether she played those games with Toshi like he said. At one point, the pressure of these demands grew so great I was afraid the questions would fly out my nose if I kept my lips sealed, but I held on, convinced I'd learn more just by listening. By the last night of our visit, I had figured out enough about the conniving ways of adults and teenagers to arrive at the answers by myself: I'd been such a little kid, to believe Toshi. He'd said it just to trick me. But I didn't have time to dwell on the profundity of this realization, because Haruna was speaking almost exactly the same lines that I'd scripted for her in my fantasy:

"I would have loved to come live with you. Your parents are great. But I can't stand it here. And I can't stand it at home. I'm going back in the fall, but if they don't let me see my boyfriend, I'm going to run away again. You're the only person who knows. Don't tell."

TELLING MY PARENTS

I decided to tell my parents that Toshi had abused me. The notion came to me a few weeks after I returned from D.C., while I was biking home from the gym in the quickening dusk. Suddenly, the reason my disclosure had caused me such distress seemed clear: I was probably right all these years in thinking that my sexual abuse had not been that big a deal, but I had given the story of it away to the wrong person. Considering how disparagingly she had talked about my mother, it was unfair that Rebecca had knowledge about me that my own mother did not. Telling my mom would be an attempt to reestablish the right balance.

As for my father, he and Rebecca talked regularly, and she was bound to share her version of the evening with him. Wouldn't he rather hear it from me? After all, learning about his wedding from her had hollowed me, left me feeling bereft. And I wouldn't want him to go through that. We were bumbling through this transition in our relationship, and we had to minimize harm where we could. I, for a change, would model the better behavior. I would tell him. My legs pumped stronger, resolute.

Then a flare of frantic aversion shot through me. I'd never spoken a single

169

word about sex or my body to my father. I avoided speaking personally about these things even to my mother. But a sense of grim duty suppressed my panic. I had no choice, some inner voice intoned.

Once home, I muscled my bike up the porch steps with unusual force.

"I decided I have to tell my parents," was my greeting to Monique.

"Are you ready?" she asked, like she already knew the answer.

"Yes."

DURING THE PAST weeks, I had come to believe that all these years I'd been making a rational decision to shield my parents from what had happened between me and Toshi. However not-that-bad I had considered the abuse, however far outside the basic sexual assault mold I thought it fell, however layered my perception was, certainly my parents would not see it that way. No caring parents want their little daughter to be touched by a boy-man. No caring parents could stand the thought of their preschooler with a hard dick in her hand, in her face, with a face in her crotch. No caring parents could face the fact that they'd invited the offender into their home. On some level I might even have defined the experience as no big deal for my parents' sakes. This analysis made me proud—of my strength, of my insight, of my ability to recognize or even create nuance, of my disinclination to cry. But we were all going to have to deal with it now. I might be reluctant to try psychotherapy, but I accepted some of its dictums, as I understood them. In the effort to heal, bringing all issues out into the open was always best.

Since I left home for college, my dad has called me every Sunday I wasn't traveling, dependable as the calendar, braving my occasional indifference or distraction and saving us from the kind of bitter fights my mother and I have over who should call whom when. I'd already talked to him since I returned from D.C., gingerly asking him if he was indeed getting married over Thanksgiving. He'd gingerly told me that no, they were going to get married sometime in the next year, but they didn't have a date set. Rebecca must have misunderstood. Would he please keep me informed? I'd requested. Of course, he'd said. The exchange hadn't done much to fill my hollows. There was a pile of unvoiced tension building up between us, and I was about to add to it now.

It was rare for me to call him on a weeknight, but I didn't want to wait.

Monique stepped into her room to give the illusion of privacy, and I stretched the cord of our phone down the hallway and into my workroom. I sat on my office chair while I dialed his number, my back to the world map I had taped on the wall, color-coded pins marking where I had been and where I hoped still to go.

When my dad heard my voice, his expression of happy surprise ended with a question mark due to the unusual day and hour.

I spoke calmly. I wanted to be reasonable, rational—we were the matched pair in our family of four when it came to handling emotion.

"I didn't tell you on Sunday, but something else came up at Rebecca's that contributed to me feeling so upset. I hadn't been planning to tell her. I hadn't been planning to tell anyone in the family. But she was talking a lot about Morris's family and asking questions about when Toshi lived with us, and I ended up telling her that Toshi molested me during the time he was there."

"Oh my God . . . Oh my God . . . I'm terribly sorry that happened." His voice was stricken.

My instinct was to pull him—us—back from an abyss. My father consistently looked for the good in people and for the silver lining, the twist that made a prognosis less grim. The Democrats might have lost the presidency, but they gained seats in the House; my hours at work might be grueling, but it sure sounded like I was doing something worthwhile. He was apparently too stunned to look on the bright side now, as perhaps I had expected him to do (but how?), so I volunteered.

"He didn't . . . rape me or anything. There was nothing violent."

"I don't know what to say or what questions to ask or anything."

"I don't know either. It just seemed wrong for Rebecca to know and not you. She didn't mention it, did she?"

"No. No, she . . . I'm glad you told me. I just . . ."

We both sat on the line.

"Well, I'm pissed off, for one thing!" I didn't recognize his manly, angry tone. It felt false to me. I didn't know what would have felt true. I had not envisioned a preferred response. I stared at the blank computer screen in front of me until we ended the call, saying we'd talk more on Sunday.

"How'd it go?" Monique asked when I went into the kitchen with a cigarette.

"Okay, I guess," I said. I shrugged. I flicked my ash and took another inhale. The clarity, the hope I'd felt on my bike ride, had already receded. Numbness took its place. "He said he was sorry. He said he was pissed. He didn't know what to say." My bowels were achy. I crushed out the cigarette although there was more than an inch till the filter. The paper ripped and the tobacco bled out. "I have to call my mom."

WHEN I TOLD HER, the first thing she said was, "But you weren't even in kindergarten yet." She sounded skeptical.

"I know."

"It seems so . . . innocent, in a way."

"I was four. He was what? Sixteen, seventeen?"

"I could see if you were older, but what was the appeal? You wouldn't even have been that attractive."

This response, outrageous though it was, put me on familiar ground. My mom's offhand ranking of my—of anyone's—physical appeal was typical of her. I might have been standing with my hand on the doorknob and hearing her say: "You're going to wear your hair like that?" Or sitting on a bench with her at the mall, where she'd interrupt me mid-sentence: "Now she's attractive. Look at her. Wow."

"Well, Mom, I don't know what to say. I'm not making this up. Apparently there was some appeal to him. I don't know if he was practicing for a girlfriend, or if he has a sickness, or what. Some people do. He told me it was a game he played with Haruna."

"Did you tell your dad?"

"Yeah, I just talked to him."

"What did he say?"

"Not too much. He said he was pissed off."

"What did Rebecca say?"

"I didn't want to talk about it with her. I felt like it was pried out of me, but I don't know. I don't know why I blurted it out."

"Have you heard from her since?"

"No."

My mom made a disapproving noise with her mouth. "Toshi was always such a strain on our family. Is Dad going to confront him?"

"We didn't talk about that."

"He always felt responsible for Toshi. He did so much for him. And this is how he's repaid." I thought I detected some satisfaction in her tone, the pleasure of a foreshadowed plot twist finally revealing itself.

"I'm not sure what should happen. But I just thought you should know."

WHY HAD I believed my parents would express a deep outrage on my behalf, that their feelings would have a clarity that would give a shape to my own? I had read enough in the psychology and recovery aisles, and even in literature, to know that responses to descriptions of sexual assault seldom yielded this result. I knew how common it was to be met with disbelief, blame, accusation. I knew that the offending family member was sometimes the one who was eventually protected and sided with. I hadn't received any of these blows, and for that I was grateful, genuinely grateful—I could be counted among the lucky ones. But I felt like I hadn't received much of anything else, either. The secret was out, and it didn't matter.

When I rejoined Monique in the kitchen, she turned up the music. The bass pressed against our thin walls, filled my emptiness with helium. We started dancing in a floaty, drunken way, holding our drinks and cigarettes aloft. There in our apartment, we performed that nightlife alchemy where pleasure is the greater for the pain it's temporarily displacing.

THE NEXT DAY, I reexamined why I hadn't told my parents sooner. Instead of writing in my journal about my silence as an act of strength, after the phone calls I explained it as an act of fear: I'd been afraid that my parents would have a reaction similar to my own—muddled, uneasy, sullied with doubt—rather than the reaction I wanted to believe real sexual abuse demanded: outrage, action. By not telling my parents, I had created a place to project the pain and anger and guilt that I felt someone ought to feel if what had happened to me was indeed akin to the crimes that made pedophiles pariahs in prisons. My parents had borne my rage for me, in absentia. Now that they knew and they didn't inhabit the roles I had retroactively assigned them—wouldn't or couldn't— the whole story came back on me. I was the child and the adult, too.

And I didn't know what to do.

When Sunday rolled around and my dad made his weekly call, he offered to buy me a ticket so that I could come out to see him. I told anyone who would listen that my dad had invited me to New Mexico not in order to talk about what Toshi had done to me, but instead of talking about it. I was disappointed that he seemed to have nothing to say, but the truth was, I didn't look forward to such a conversation either. I kept postponing my trip. When I finally went, I was prickly, throwing up all my defenses. I did nothing to broach the topic of Toshi, and neither did he.

WHEN MY MOM tried to bring it up later, I responded coldly. I didn't want to talk.

MY FATHER and his partner didn't end up getting married that year after all. When they had a wedding the year after that, Rebecca wasn't there. I don't know if she ever spoke to my father about our conversation at her house. As far as my family was concerned, the issue went back underground soon after I brought it up.

For me, though, it remained on the surface. I thought about the sexual abuse and where it fit in my family, crafting theory after theory and story after story in an effort to find one that made sense. I dreamt about it, several times visioning a small girl made of green smoke who needed me to carry her to safety. And I wrote about it. Cigarette lit, bourbon at my elbow. Fall came, then winter moved closer, the keyboard went *clackclackclackclack*.

But even more often than I wrote about Toshi and my family, I wrote about my romantic relationship and my sex life. These topics were easier and more fun for me, something I noted explicitly and that's evident in the omissions in the pages. After I came back from the visit with my father, I made short work of the trip and instead described in great detail several occasions where Tom and I had not been in synch sexually, times when I'd had a strong negative reaction to his trying to seduce me after I'd expressed an uncommon disinterest, or when I'd been repulsed by an attempt of his to go down on me. Might this have anything to do with Toshi? I asked in my journal. I didn't think so. I was more interested in considering how my reactions fit into gendered patterns and whether they signaled the disintegration of the relationship. Tom and I were reaching our end.

WHEN I REDISCOVERED the journal from this time a few years ago, I braced myself as I opened up the binder of printed-out pages, expecting to cringe at the overwrought analysis or sweeping generalizations of a self-absorbed younger me, as I sometimes do reading through old notebooks. But I didn't have this reaction. In general, I found the pages to be written by an adult.

Since I could remember, I had been eager for adulthood, had rushed toward every milestone of independence. But it's clear to me now that it wasn't until around the time of this telling that I actually reached full maturity. My sense of self was becoming more intrinsic, less dependent on being a parented person. I could see greater nuance in how I related to the world.

THREE

FAMILY

I was proud of myself for separating from Tom without having another man lined up to take his place, and I needed that pride to sustain me through some wintry nights alone. Soon after my breakup, Monique met someone with whom she fell almost instantly in love. My other close friends were coupled up, too. I had what I'd said I'd wanted, time to read for sustained periods and sit alone at my computer, but without an active sexual relationship I felt out in the cold. When I heard Monique jangling at the door, I'd rush from my writing room to meet her. We'd sit at our table and talk for an hour or two before she headed out to take the bus up to Jason's place, and our conversations now included long descriptions of him, of his artwork, his aesthetic, his distinction, his manner in bed, his mystique. I felt the wistfulness of a best friend displaced, and it didn't help when, probably noticing this, Monique started telling me about Jason's roommate Anthony.

"He's very intriguing. He and Jason are just like us, best friends who live together."

One afternoon she came home and held up the book I had set on the table, *Butterfly Stories* by William T. Vollmann.

"I can't believe it! Anthony is reading this, too!" She was giddy.

"He's probably a big Vollmann fan, part of the cult," I said dismissively. "I'm not at all. I just happen to like this book."

Though irritated by Monique's cheerleading for Anthony, I agreed that we could invite him and Jason over for dinner. When our buzzer rang, I let Monique rush to greet them while I took a seat on the hot grill of the space heater, aloof. But before the door had even closed behind the men, I was intrigued. Anthony was tall, thin, and spiky-haired; he wore a leather jacket. But his bad boy vibe swirled with something sweet as he bent way down to pet the cats who twined around his legs, then gave me a crinkly eyed smile.

OUR FIRST DATE was long and boozy, our conversation roaming widely in the three hours we sat facing each other, eyes mostly locked. The next day was Valentine's Day, and I grinned each time I put a candy heart into my mouth, the messages exemplifying my mood: *Wow! Hot stuff!* But we went out two more times before we even kissed. I had never proceeded so slowly and yet with such certitude, and by the time we leaned toward each other on the bench seat of his gigantic old Buick after a dinner of Vietnamese food, I already liked him a lot. It was freezing outside, and I had a hat and scarf and thick parka on, no skin at all available to be touched, but the communication of just our mouths and breath reached deep inside of my winter armor. We kissed until the heat generated by the car dissipated and the warmth came only from us. We could feel the chill if we moved even a few inches beyond our bubble, and so we pressed even closer. The fog on the windows turned to frost. We made a plan to go out again on Tuesday.

"I haven't thought about anything but kissing you since Sunday," Anthony said as soon as he picked me up. "Can we kiss again before we go anywhere?" So we made out in his car some more, smiling through some of it, a little more sex mixed into the communion, until eventually we pulled away long enough for him to turn the key in the ignition and float us through the slushy streets to a bar we'd planned to try. It was one of those places that had expanded to include an adjoining apartment, with a tub still in the women's bathroom, a pool table in what used to be the living room, and couches in the former bedrooms. We sat on one of those, and despite our pre-game go, we couldn't exchange more than a few sentences before we found ourselves kissing again, for the first time without coats on. Bodies! Limbs! The warmth of his big hands burned through my sweater. Our pint glasses sat still two-thirds full, but we were drunk, our self-consciousness puddled at our feet.

Maybe we should just forget finishing the beers and go back to my place now.

I think that's what I meant to say when I came up for breath, but instead I blurted, "I was molested when I was little. I just thought you should know."

"Okay," he said. Frank and open.

"I don't think it damaged me or anything, but I'm not sure. It's been on my mind. But I don't know why I said that just now." My heart thumped in my chest and my skin burned where his hand rested on my thigh. I was rushing my words as if taking a happy plunge, as if I'd asked him back to my place instead of suggesting I might be someone with trauma-born sex hangups.

"Should we stop?" The right question.

"No!"

WE NEVER DID FINISH our beers. We went back to my futon and took off our clothes for real. I felt the gleeful, careless happiness possible when there's mad mutual attraction without any defensive entwining, when everything's been pleasure and nothing yet has hurt.

"I can't believe I just blurted it out like that," I said a few months later. We were already making the stories of our meeting into legend—the drinks we'd ordered on our first date, the gay bar he'd taken me to on our second, the complaint he made about his scratchy sweater that he used as an excuse to take off his clothes. And my weirdly timed admission of having been sexually abused. "What was I thinking?"

"I have no idea. Maybe you were trying to scare me away."

"But all I wanted to do was go to bed with you! Did you feel scared?"

"I felt bad for you. But I didn't feel shocked."

"Maybe it was some kind of test?"

"I hope I passed."

"You totally passed," I said, kissing him. "Even if I don't know what."

We were at the stage of our relationship where we could talk for hours about the minutiae of our childhoods, the alternating paucity or grandiosity of our dreams, the moments of personal revelation that had shown us as either more or less than we hoped to be. I found I could speak about the abuse without each word escaping from behind an electrical fence, or without seeing myself from a great distance, trying out a claim or complaint I wasn't sure I owned. In part, the topic was easier to linger on now that there was a new chapter to the story. I acknowledged what had happened when I was four and five, but—because who wanted to linger there?—mostly I talked about what led me to tell my parents and what had (not) happened when I did. And if my broaching this topic in some detail was, despite my knowing it, another test, Anthony passed it again. He was right where I needed him to be at that time. He took my side but without any macho posturing. He neither dismissed me nor took the situation more seriously than I did myself. He expressed some concerned interest but he did not probe. The murky part of my past in which my teenaged cousin had assaulted me in my childhood bed seemed to take its rightful place, out in the open but in a corner that didn't need to be cleared to make room for any dancing.

We dated for about a year and a half before we moved in together, and then it was another year and some months before we decided to get married. My father was the first person we told. We both agreed we wanted it to be him. We knew that he would give us the most exuberant blessing.

WE PLANNED A SMALL wedding in Santa Fe, at a chapel that could only fit the two dozen people we invited if most of them stood during the ceremony. The distance from home and the small size of the venue was intentional. It gave us an excuse to keep the guest list limited to only the people with whom we felt most intimate. In conversation with my father, my cousin Haruna expressed interest in attending the wedding with her husband—like everyone else, they'd be flying in from another state, giving over several days in our honor. But I said no when my father asked me hopefully if we'd consider inviting her. And I said no again when he reposed the question again a couple weeks later. It was unusual for him to press an issue, and, knowing this, it was unusual for me not to cede to him the rare times he did, but I felt strongly about this. Though I had positive memories of Haruna, that branch of the family cast a shadow that I didn't want darkening the celebration, and I wanted my father's full attention on the new relatives we were gaining through marriage.

EVERYTHING ABOUT our wedding went according to plan, conforming to or even expanding our fantasy of it. When Monique helped me get ready, she gave me a necklace she had made that transformed my wedding costume into something thoroughly mine. Anthony and I had consulted a solar calculator so that we could time the ending of our ceremony with the sunset, and the chapel portico did indeed glow with a golden purple light when we drank our first sips of married champagne. Our fathers—both born in Western Pennsylvania to immigrant parents—did indeed take to each other. The musicians played far longer into the night than we had hired them to. Everyone enjoyed the Grand Marnier that flowed freely after dinner, but no one got too sloppily drunk. We drove off in a red convertible to our honeymoon in the San Juan range of the Rockies, and we spent hours once ensconced in Ouray just gazing at the fierce, young peaks that surrounded the town, basking in the feeling that we were creating ourselves as a family, melding what we wanted from the past into something new. As if this were alchemy we could control. As if our families started and stopped where we said they did.

It was a beautiful week.

My son collects pocket knives. I told him about the time on a Girl Scout campout when I disobeyed the common rule of whittling, the demonstrated knowledge of which had helped me earn me a badge, and pulled my knife towards me rather than away while fashioning a tin can camp stove. I cut a quarter-inch chunk of flesh off the edge of my thumb, along with a crescent of nail. Knowing that I shouldn't have been carving that way, I kept quiet about the wound. I took my bandana down to the pump and soaked it with cold water, wrapped it tightly around my finger. Every few minutes I glanced down to see how far the blood had soaked through, making excuses to go back to the pump and rinse out the cloth when it was saturated, to wrap it tight round again. No one noticed. The throbbing in my hand thumped loud as a drumbeat through my whole body, but that made me steady. In the tent that night, I unwrapped the bandana and showed my friends the gash, their flashlights trained on it. I borrowed another bandana and kept pressing. By morning the bleeding had slowed enough so that I could use Band-Aids to staunch the stream. I used all those in my first aid kit as well as my friends'. The scar was gone by the time I had kids, so I had no visual to offer them, but the story was dramatic enough to garner their interest all the same. I don't see it as a tale that offers a clear moral. My instinct tells me that I can build my children's trust by sometimes offering stories that don't.

But then I second-guess the merits of that approach.

"I want you to know," I told my son, "I won't get mad at you if you come to me with an injury. I might lecture you, but it's worth one lecture to make sure you don't make anything worse."

"Okay," he said.

I hope that when push comes to shove he won't sneak around if he's hurt, no matter the cause. Even if that's not exactly what my stories caution.

WHEN I WAS A TEENAGER, and after I had already gotten into and been punished for a few dramatically drunken or brazen scrapes, my parents decided that my honesty and safety should be paramount, more important than rules. For instance, if I needed a ride somewhere because the driver I was with had been drinking, I was to call them and let them know. I wouldn't get in trouble for being at a gathering where there was alcohol. This arrangement was predicated on their sense that my hunger for teenage thrill was natural and probably too keen to thwart—look what had happened when my uncle had tried to box his kids in, after all—but that I was also fundamentally level-headed, a view supported by my dutiful completion of AP-level homework and my responsibility at any job I took.

I pushed it with my parents. Itchy for change and adventure, I was a hard partier in high school. I remember being drunk past midnight one night—there were many such nights—and calling from a phone booth to ask them to come pick me up, probably more out of convenience than anything else. They'd been sleeping when I rang. When the tone of my mom's voice veered toward anger, I played the trump card: but you told me to always be honest, not to get in the car with someone who was drunk.

And if I was honest about where I was going, I'd wave that like a truce flag to outlaw any incoming no's. One weekend, I told them as I left the house that I was heading to a co-ed sleepover at a male friend's. When the host's parents returned on Sunday and deduced there'd been a bacchanal, they called the homes of everyone they'd gotten their son to name to encourage parents

to take some recourse. When my dad explained his and my mother's position over the phone to the other dad, a longtime friend of theirs, the other
parent's angry skepticism filled our kitchen. Isn't it a parent's job to ensure
that their kids aren't running amock, copulating drunkenly? Weren't we too
young to handle these things? And who wants to think about their kids drinking and drugging and groping each other anyway?

I don't. I was twelve when I started drinking. My oldest is eleven as I
write this. The thought of my children doing what I did in those early years,
especially, is almost impossible to fathom. I tell myself that we live in a different kind of place than the one where I grew up, where there's more to do
than get a buzz on. But I think my parents' logic was fundamentally correct:
if they were to have any chance of punishing and restricting me into partying
less, we would have had to fight and I would have had to lie a lot more. By
senior year, my parents and I were good friends, and my binge drinking was
largely behind me at an age when many American kids were just gearing up
to go at it. Was this due to good parenting or good luck?

ACCORDING TO ANN HULBERT's book *Raising America*, which puts
child-rearing schools into a historical context, very little of advice coming
from so-called parenting experts is scientifically born out. Hubert provides
evidence that the philosophies of the best-selling authors in the field can be
traced to whether the authors seek to repudiate or recreate the conditions
in which they were raised, rather than to any set of facts. Among my friends
who have kids, I notice the same tendency.

In many ways, I fall into the camp of borrowing from my parents' parenting strategies—their mix of leniency and authority; their prioritization
of honesty. But I believe I've made improvements on handling issues related to the body and sexual abuse. On these topics, where the only example handed down to me is mostly an absence, I've unreservedly looked for
expert guidance. Periodically, I use bath times or bedtimes or after-dinner moments with my children to—sometimes awkwardly, sometimes
smoothly—check off items from lists like the following from the nonprofit
Darkness to Light.

- Teach your children about their bodies, about what abuse is, and, when age-appropriate, about sex. Teach them words that help them discuss sex comfortably with you.
- Model caring for your own body, and teach children how to care for theirs.
- Teach children that it is "against the rules" for adults to act in a sexual way with them and use examples. Teach them what parts of their bodies others should not touch.
- Be sure to mention that the abuser might be an adult friend, family member, or older youth.
- Start early and talk often. Use everyday opportunities to talk about sexual abuse. One survey showed that fewer than 30% of parents ever discussed sexual abuse with their children. And even then, most failed to mention that the abuser might be an adult friend or family member.
- Be proactive. If a child seems uncomfortable, or resistant to being with a particular adult, ask why.

By following these suggestions, I think I've created an opening for my children to come to me if they've been approached sexually or in a way that makes them uncomfortable. And if my children were to indicate to me that someone had trespassed their boundaries, or if I were to witness behavior that suggested sexual abuse might be occurring, I believe I'm prepared to handle it sensitively. To not turn away. To act firmly but not in a manner that would alarm them.

But even though I've cultivated in myself a pro-sex attitude and a bent toward frankness, discussing matters of sex and sexual assault with my kids hasn't come as easily to me as I would have once believed, and it took me longer to get started than it should have.

My son is much more outgoing than I am, more comfortable around adults than I ever was as a child. He'll turn his sunshine beam on anyone. Since toddlerhood, he's struck up conversations with homeless people, museum guards, authority figures, other parents. He'll happily accept social overtures from wherever they come in the rare case he hasn't made one first. I see this quality as a strength. From the time that he could speak in full sentences,

I felt a conflict between my desire not to undermine his trust in others and my pressing need to start the conversation about inappropriate touching.

He was almost five when I broached the topic for the first time, finally bringing it up one weekend in the middle of tidying the art supplies that were scattered on our dining room table. He seemed far away from me, all the way on the other side of the wide pine tabletop, which came up to his chest.

"Has any big person every tried to touch your bumbie or your testicles or your penis?"

His head barely shook. His thick hair was longish, his bangs hanging below his eyebrows and making his head look extra large on his string bean neck. He blinked up at me apprehensively and said nothing, unusual for him.

"No big person except me and Daddy and the doctor should ever ask to touch or see those parts, and you shouldn't have to touch or see theirs, okay?"

He gave a single chin-bob for a nod. His face flickered incomprehension, and then his attention turned.

"Please tell me or Daddy if someone wants to touch you there, okay? Not every adult is a good person you can trust."

It pained me to say those words to him, and his look of confusion and innocence hurt even more. At his age I had a fantasy life that included elaborate, roaming vehicles devoted to genital-based humiliations and punishments, but he appeared to have absolutely no context in which to place my statements. He seemed unable to imagine one. It was easy to believe that his very wide-heartedness would protect him, somehow. Sunshine as disinfectant. And there was that niggling sense—which I knew enough to discount but sometimes claimed with an almost-pride—that my own shadowy corners and precocious interest in sex made my childhood abuse if not forgone, then more likely.

When my son was in first grade and in the chess club, we received a notice from the school district that they'd been contacted by the FBI about one of the chess coaches. Apparently, the feds had intercepted some letters that he'd sent to an incarcerated friend, which included sexual references to children and photographs of kids on the chess team—fully dressed and engaged in matches—with lewd statements written above some of their heads.

Although many parents had gotten a weird vibe from the coach, who'd been in the military and had a strange intensity to him, the kids universally loved him. The district and the principal had been very responsive to the news they'd received, informing the parents in a systematic way, meeting personally with those whose children were included in the photographs, but they left us largely on our own to deal with our kids' reaction to losing their coach. When the news came down after a couple weeks of his absence that he wouldn't ever be coming back, my son sobbed.

"Why?" he cried, body shaking. "Why? He was the best coach ever!"

In the face of his pain and my alternation between panic at what had almost happened and near-disbelief about what had, I grew frantic.

"They found some letters where he was saying bad things about some of the kids. The police thought he was probably going to do bad things to kids." My tone was urgent and pleading.

"But he was always so nice to us!"

"Sometimes a grown-up acts that way so the kids won't understand they're going to do something bad. I'm so sorry that this is true, but not all adults can be trusted!"

"I don't understand! Even if he did something wrong, why don't they give him one more chance?"

"The school and the grown-ups who care about you can't take any chances when it comes to protecting you. We have to watch out!"

I couldn't go farther in my explanation, even as I felt like I was blowing my chance to get this right, to impart important knowledge. I had given my son all the words, but I couldn't utter them in relation to an adult he'd admired: genitals, testicles, butts, penises. He was shy about using these words even in relation to his own self-care.

"Why can't we even say goodbye?" The injustice overwhelmed him and his crying mounted. I put my arms around him, and we crumbled down together so he could wipe his snot and tears on the knee of my jeans.

UNFORTUNATELY, I HAD a chance to improve on my response a couple years later, when another well-liked coach was dismissed for asking kids during a travel tournament to come hang out in his hotel room. The kids hadn't been under the coach's purview at the tournament. The oldest among them felt suspicious enough about the invitation to report to his mom, who reported it to the other children's parents and to the principal at school.

When I tried to talk to my son frankly about why he couldn't see the coach again, his eyes glazed over. He never expressed any curiosity when it came to matters of sex. He practiced outright avoidance whenever I tried to bring the subject up.

But he was old enough, and the situation was specific enough, that I felt I could talk to him. I felt like I had to.

"Listen, this stuff really happens. Something like that happened to me when I was around your age."

His head jerked up, his eyes wide. "What?"

I DIDN'T TELL HIM about Toshi. I told him about the time a friend and I had been roaming around the deserted student union building on the college campus on a summer afternoon, playing hide and seek in the same echoey halls I would later walk down on my way to violin lessons. A middle-aged white man had been the only other person we'd seen in the building, and it did seem strange, the way he was strolling with his hands jangling in his pockets down the same out-of-the-way corridors we were, but we felt we owned that campus in the summer breaks, and we were in the thick of our game; it didn't occur to us to stop. His comments were innocuous enough, as was his comb-over, his pale face and pocket shirt. Just an annoying grown-up. Until eventually, he cornered me as I was getting a drink at a fountain by a restroom, and when I turned around, he grabbed my crotch and murmured something like, "What you got there?"

"Don't!" I batted his hand and sidestepped him, ran to the center of the building, a two-story lobby flanked by banks of entrance doors.

"Jennifer! Jennifer! Come out!" I yelled to my friend, breaking the still air where our footsteps had been the loudest thing. And there she was.

Her dad Biff came to pick us up moments later, and we told him what happened. I could see him do calculations, switch into a different mode. He was a short, broad, quiet man, with a carton of Luckies and a gun rack in his Jeep.

"And there he is, Daddy," my friend said in a voice meant to be heard. We weren't powerless anymore. We weren't alone. We had a man, too. "That man, there." He was slipping out of the building, and as she pointed he picked up his pace down the broad cement stairs.

"Hey!" Biff called, more a grunt than a word. "Hey, you stop right there!" He started after the crotch-grabber, went halfway down the flight, but the other man was moving as quickly as he could without outright running—the clank of his change reached our ears— and Biff would have had to fully engage in a chase to catch up. And then what? I could see him ask the question of himself, think the better of it. He had to be more dad than avenger; he had to stay with us. He walked me in to my house instead of dropping me off, and he talked to my parents. Together, they called the police. Two came quickly. They listened to me soberly, one sketching as I talked.

"Does this look about right?"

"Sort of," I said. "Maybe his glasses were darker. Yeah."

I GAVE MY SON most of these details. I even used the word *crotch*, which sounded vulgar in his proximity. "And a little while later, maybe a few weeks, maybe a couple months, they caught him raping a girl in a parking lot," I told my son. "It's a terrible thing, but you have to know. Bad people are out there."

We looked into each other's eyes. Serious. I saw that he heard me. He'd wanted to protect himself from knowing this, from knowing anything about these shadows, and up until then he'd been able to, but he let me in with my dark knowledge. It made me happy. It made me sad.

When it comes to talking about body parts and their uses and potential for invasion, my daughter is quite different from my son. She's explicitly curious about how she works, about where poop and pee and babies come from, about how babies get in there and fit on the way out. I started talking to her about protecting herself much earlier than I did to her brother. She gleefully recites the protective mantras in the bath.

"No one should ever touch my bumbie. That's private! No one should ever touch my vulva. If anyone ever tries, I'll tell them: NO! And then I'll tell you!" She shouts this out triumphantly.

"That's right!" I say, sounding as adamant as she does. It makes me happy to hear her, even though all the ways in which her statements are not literally true rise up in me, make me face my conflicting obligations as a parent: to protect my child from sexual abuse and allow her a shame-free enjoyment of her own sexuality. And of course some people should touch her butt and vulva, someday. She'll want them to. She'll want them to so badly that the world will consist of just that need, a spreading desire as burning and lit as lava, with the potential to change her landscape forever. I see her naked, spark-plug, certain self in the bath and I see her future self too, or sense her—womanly, crackling, oceanic, ghostly, with a well of sexual urges and experiences that I'll never be privy to no matter how close we might be when she reaches adulthood. I want to commune with both these presences right now, somehow, or to protect them both. But there's no place in the conversation about the privacy of a four-year-old's bumbie and vulva for a discussion of scalding desire.

But I know not to talk about it in this context. I know that. I practice acting as if I know that so it will become my truth.

"That's right," I say again. "Except a doctor or a nurse if they have to for your health."

ADAMANCY IS CHARACTERISTIC of my daughter. She's always looking for rules of nature and making pronouncements. She doesn't ask questions so much as pose truths. "Mama," she'll state. "The blood is on your bones, and blood is really heavy on there, and the most blood is in your leg right here because this is the heaviest part of me, and if I get a cut there the blood will *goosh!*" If I don't offer instant confirmation—and I seldom do, my mind reeling back from wherever it was to try to sort through the logic of her statement, to identify my responsibilities in helping her learn—she'll fish: "Right?"

"Mama. I don't need to be afraid of wolves because nice wolves will know I'm not afraid and they are friends with people who aren't, because not being afraid of them is what makes them nice."

A pause while I cease calculating the worth of paying to park closer to the office so that I can be sure to make the meeting on time and shift to wondering if I'm endangering her if I let her think that wild wolves might in any circumstance be friendly, that in general being friendly is always a good.

"Right?"

I think I can let this one slide.

"Right, sweetie. Come on. Hop out. Let's go to school."

Her totems are the wolf and the bear. Hunters. Fighters. Although, she wants to love on them; she's fiercely affectionate. She knocks me down with her embraces, grinds her face into mine when we kiss. Our cuddle sessions come with anxiety for me because I know the likelihood of physical pain is imminent. She's big for her age, and mashes too hard.

My totem is some kind of bird. Not a regal, glorious bird of prey. Something midsized, bony, nervous, quick. Able to see the wide view—all the literal and figurative ways in which a belief that fearlessness leads to friendships might play out—but not often comfortable alighting too close to others for long.

WHEN MY SON was in his first year of middle school, I went to a PTA meeting about substance abuse. My attendance was only half-intentional. It had been on my radar as something I should do to signal to myself my own desire to parent a tweenager responsibly, but I probably would have skipped it, as I did most such things despite the nag of good intentions, if my son hadn't been at school that evening for another reason. I slipped into the meeting midstream when I went to pick him up.

I waited impatiently for the items of business to be completed—the status of the library renovation fund-raising project, a discussion about entering a corporate-sponsored app-building contest. If I didn't get home within an hour, I'd either miss putting my daughter to bed or she'd stay up too late and be cranky in the morning. Finally, the expert from the substance abuse nonprofit took the floor, a woman who had not yet entered middle age but was dressed as if she had, in a white blouse under a burgundy sweater, a black skirt that came to her knees. She clicked through some slides of data that had been published repeatedly in the community paper—how many students at what age smoke cigarettes, smoke weed, drink, do drugs. I squirmed in my seat and looked at the clock again, shifting from striver-mom wannabe mode into empathizing with the kids: this is boring. I've heard it before.

The presenter clicked to a slide that broke down the data on hard drug use. Her chart showed virtually no use of heroin in the local student community, although I knew from a friend that several high school students had recently overdosed and/or gone to rehab for addiction to it. I didn't want to let this go unsaid, compelled on some level to demonstrate my street-level cool by revealing an awareness of hardcore drug use. It was as if I was still a twenty-year-old in anarcho-punk Philadelphia, as if I weren't a mom at a PTA meeting sweating in a Patagonia parka about all the ways in which she might not be sufficiently scaffolding her kids to succeed and be safe. I raised my hand, and when I was called on I brought up the conflict between my first-hand knowledge and the charts on the screen. Another woman in the audience, her highlighted blond hair swinging along her jawline, quickly added that actually, based on her teenaged experience, the numbers in general seemed almost low. I felt a swell of fraternity with her and wished she and I were discussing this over a cocktail.

The presenter fought back by reiterating her statistics and saying that her office worked with student surveys and local law enforcement to derive them, and then she advanced the PowerPoint to another aspect of the discussion. This slide, too, had been reproduced in the community paper. It told parents what they can do to lower the chances that their children will use drugs or alcohol: keep track of your own supply, since most kids start drinking booze they pilfer from their parents. If you don't drink regularly, pour out or give away alcohol left over from parties or events, because it's too ripe for the picking. Communicate very clearly to your children that drinking and drugs are harmful and that their use is absolutely not acceptable.

She raised her small voice to emphasize the last point. She spoke in italics.

"We know there is a *direct, documented* correlation between parents stating *explicitly* that they will not tolerate drinking or drug use and students' rate of use." She was stern, making eye contact with her audience in a way that left me feeling accused. "In adolescence, brain development is not yet complete. Drinking and drug use have a *much* greater impact than they will later on."

"But don't we want them to be able to come to us? If there's zero tolerance, aren't they going to be afraid to tell us what's really going on?" The wide-bottomed woman with a river of wavy hair who asked the question cocked her head slightly, seemed willing to engage in a debate.

"The research is not ambiguous on this point. Teenagers who say that their parents will not tolerate drugs or alcohol use at far lower rates."

My husband and I had already let my son take a taste of beer. Anthony had told him that his cousins in Italy drink a watered-down wine at dinner, even kids his age.

"Well, what do we say when our kids ask about our own experiences?" the woman continued. "I don't really want to lie, and . . ."

The presenter visibly inhaled and exhaled. "If you're not comfortable with not telling the truth, you can deflect and say, 'What's important is that *you* don't do this, because it's damaging.' Because when they're asking you what you did, that's not really what they want to know. They're actually asking you what *they* should do. And you need to be clear."

A snake of cold slipped through me. Deflecting interest my son showed in me, let alone lying to him, went against my inherent parenting style. Not that I wanted to tell my eleven-year-old son that I started drinking when I was twelve. But I wanted that connection we sometimes had when he seemed to realize I wasn't always a mom, that I'd been a kid. In part, I sought this connection because I thought it would help him open up to me, trust me, see me as someone who has relevant advice to give, to not feel alone. And in part I sought it just because I wanted to be seen by someone I love. Was this selfish?

If the cold, prim presenter was getting to me—and she was, well beyond the scope of the topic—it was because in its broad sense this question about the motivation for telling unsavory truth was one I was sitting with every day as I mulled over writing this book, and she was offering an institutional answer to it: yes, telling the truth was selfish when it comes to children, and if I wanted the best for mine, I might have to give it up. The conclusion I was jumping to was that she—"they," "everyone," even my husband at times, though he was reluctant to show it—thought that shutting up about the messy stuff was what a responsible, right-thinking person, or parent at least, does, because responsible, right-thinking, never-in-distress or too-far-off-the-path people are what we're looking to turn out.

Even over a decade after having my son, the expectation that parents are central to healthy character-forming tripped me up. Of course I wanted a child healthy in every way. But before I had children—especially in my formative years, but even as my own middle-class impulses began to emerge—I sought out places where it was okay to be bad, or odd, or weird, or dirty, or just generally outside the mainstream. That was where I was comfortable, even if I myself didn't choose to act out. That was where I found interest, and truth. The family-oriented environs of the desirable community Anthony and I had moved to was decidedly not one of those places, and it sometimes left me feeling like an imposter.

Most of the time I was comfortable in my parenting, in myself. But then these waves of anxiety swept over me. What it came down to, I suppose, is that I was worried that I would raise a kid like myself, and also that I wouldn't.

I WAS COMPLETELY rattled by the time I left the PTA meeting, my son at my side. We walked to the car together, the grass smelling of a cold thaw. Even in my nervous state, I registered the pleasure I took in matching our newly twinned, quick strides. Because of the dark and the cold and the tiredness that was already descending on me when I left home, I'd driven to the meeting although the school is only about five blocks away from our house. My son walked there himself every morning. He walked to elementary school by himself the previous couple years as well, one of the first kids his age to do so. I was proud of his independence; glad he wanted it, glad to give it. Unlike some parents, his setting off alone never terrified me. I'd watch him fondly, with his big backpack and little stocking cap, stepping lightly off into the world with a mix of boyish zing and self-possession.

In the car I asked him about how much he had paid attention to the meeting. I relayed to him the statistics about how many sixth and seventh grade students were drinking and smoking weed. "Have you tried any of that?" I asked. "Do you know anyone who has?" I tried to keep my voice judgment free.

He was aghast. "No!" When I pressed him a little, he became agitated. "Mom, look at who I'm friends with. My friends are *nice*."

I felt a flash of defensiveness. Was he saying me and my friends weren't nice? Or was my reaction just annoyance at his show of credulity?

I decided to slap together my own impulses towards transparency and disclosure with the presenter's hard line on tolerating substance use. "If you would have asked me before tonight what I had thought about teenagers drinking, I would have said it was no big deal to have some beer or whatever before you were twenty-one. That it's normal. But this woman was saying that my attitude could be harmful to you. That when you're a teenager, your brain is still growing and that there are greater risks than I realize."

I heard myself yammering on, my voice pitched higher than usual. Before I was twenty-one I had criss-crossed the country on Greyhound buses and my upturned thumb; established myself in England; tromped through

Amsterdam, Hamburg, Berlin, and Barcelona, half in the bag half of the time on a variety of substances. I don't blame my parents for any of this. I thank my parents. Not only did I not follow American laws when it came to drugs and alcohol, I wouldn't have wanted to hang out with anyone who did. What a hypocrite.

But my son didn't ask me what I did when I was young. I considered the bargain the presenter's words implied—that if anything happens to him it's all my fault; that if I accept this responsibility, nothing ever will. How seductive, but how stressful. Maybe I didn't blame my parents for anything because I didn't want to be blamed.

We'd arrived home and stepped out of the car onto our dirt driveway.

"Can we make a deal?" I said. "While you live with us, you will follow the laws about drinking and drugs."

"Deal," he agreed. Anything to shut me up.

By the time I reached my early thirties, I'd grown more comfortable with my memories of sex abuse and with my parents' imperfections. I had formed an identity that felt solid, a firm sense of myself as a writer, worker, partner, and woman. But the thought of becoming a mother—responsible for a child's well-being, his or her very life—called all this into question. Anthony and I had known we'd wanted kids, and when I got pregnant it'd been planned, we'd been trying, but it still took me two missed periods to acknowledge what was happening in my body. I maintained some ambivalence right up to my due date.

But then I birthed my son and the love and anxiety and milk and hormones and the pulsing certainty of our relationship obliterated my doubt and remove. I had never been so present. This was agonizing during the long hours of the baby's flailing and screaming, but he cried least when he was strapped to my body while I was walking, and so that's how we spent great chunks of that springtime. He was born in April, and as we clocked miles through the neighborhood and along the lakefront, I watched the leaves and flowers bud, and I breathed in the damp earth with the scent of his baby head.

Every little infant-wear ducky decal and lamb appliqué made sense to me finally. The very universe made a new kind of sense. I was in accord—that is, I and Anthony and our baby were—with the robin red breasts flitting back to their nests and the boughs of narcissus sending out their blooms, with the tilt of the earth and the turn of the seasons.

On these walks I sometimes wondered whether my years of questioning social norms had been a waste of time. This elemental maternal happiness was not to become a hallmark of mine—it seldom lasted even until evening—but to take on the role of caregiver in the cycle of life felt profound, no matter my other emotions.

THIS WAS MY STATE when Anthony and I took our first flight with the baby and went to see my family in Albuquerque. It was toward the end of that week-long visit that my mother told me Toshi had been arrested for child sexual assault and was awaiting trial, and that my father had helped to take him from Chiyo. To contain that information was excruciating for me, but it seemed untenable to speak of it, even, beyond a few whispered phrases, to Anthony. The baby was almost always in our arms, and although he was too young to understand what we said, I'd seen evidence that he picked up on our emotions. I didn't want to contaminate him with this ugliness. Nor did I want my mom to overhear any conversation between Anthony and me. I didn't trust her to be sensitive to my feelings when my own instinct was not to treat them delicately but rather to punish them, to abrade them under my feet so they'd wrench apart and scatter, unrecognizable. Even if I could speak to Anthony privately, I wasn't sure whether I wanted him to help me with this task of destroying my own emotions or keep me from it, and I was afraid that whatever his approach, it would seem the wrong one, and I'd be left with a rift in our relationship on top of everything else.

The person I least wanted to talk to was my father. The thought of opening my mouth in his presence and letting such ugly accusations and emotions fly out made me want to throw up. It seemed possible that neither of us would be able to look at the other the same way again. But in the muddle of the blame-placing, grief-screaming, and deal-making that passed as my thoughts, I believed that failure to raise the issue with him now would be a final verdict on my complicity.

WE VISITED MY FATHER once more before heading back to Illinois. He lived on the other side of town in his wife's old adobe—a real one, not cinder blocks covered in stucco as in the newer developments such as my mother's. The house was built not to celebrate the sunlight, but to keep cool in the days before air conditioning, and it wrapped around an interior courtyard where grew a single tree. My father's wife was also a Navajo studies person, an anthropologist, and their home had the feeling of a quirky museum, some cross between the 1970s and the 1930s. The floors were covered in red tile or in shag carpeting, and the walls were decorated with Navajo rugs in the spaces between the bookshelves, some built by my father. There was a loom in the living room, and Native pottery shared the surfaces of side tables with stacks of magazine and journals.

All this was familiar to me from previous visits, but since my dad had moved in, I'd mostly slept elsewhere when I came to town. I still felt like a guest in this home. I didn't feel comfortable rummaging the fridge for a snack or opening drawers to look for a scarf to borrow. When I spied one of the stray objects that had come from the house my father and I had shared, I felt a tug. These relics highlighted both a gulf and a bond. My father had ceased smoking a pipe years ago, but in the corner of the living room where he'd made his study, he had some old Sail tobacco cans, used now to hold his spare change. Just the sight of them filled my nose with the scent of rosy tobacco, made me expect to find tobacco silt among the cache of ballpoint pens and vials of mechanical pencil lead that still hovered around his wallet the way they always had in my youth. Above his desk hung a multi-photo framed display that I had made for him one Christmas when I was in high school, back when my parents were still married. My mom had helped me select the photos that represented the broadest range of years and history. There were pictures of my brother and me as children; of my dad's parents sitting stiffly on our couch; of his brother and sister and their families, the Japanese cousins from their one visit to our home, the Pittsburgh cousins on a hike out West; and of Toshi, somewhere in the Philippines, where he'd been stationed for a while.

I'd been walking the baby around the house to soothe him, and I paused in front of the photos, looking at them for clues to my past, to this present, to a store of bravery that would let me move forward. When my dad came in from the other room to join me, I hadn't found it yet. But I tried.

"Mom mentioned something about Toshi," I said tentatively. Just five words. The effort it took me to say them left me as winded as if I had hollered.

Still, they were out there.

Gloom curtained my dad's face. His brow lowered. His voice sank. "Oh, it's a terrible thing."

"Mom told me." I didn't want to make him say more than he wanted, but I wanted him to say something. "She couldn't remember any of the details. She wasn't sure if there was more than one girl or what."

"Well, he's just being charged for one. There's a lot that's unclear."

"When did it happen? What . . . "

"Last year. I think . . . someone walked in on him."

"So he's been in jail since then, or . . ."

"He's been in jail waiting for the trial, which is happening soon. And then if he's guilty, he'll go to prison."

"I'd say there's not much question that he's guilty, Dad. We know he has a history of this."

"It's terrible. It's a tragedy. It's . . ." The indefinite pronoun acted like an eraser, smudging out my experience. Perhaps—after all, back to this—what happened to me had been no big deal.

But it—my it—had been the beginning, hadn't it? The beginning of something with a terrible end? A man in jail for sexually assaulting a girl, or girls—a number of children that was still unclear, at least to me.

I had to say something. Maybe I should I contact the prosecution and offer my history and go to court and testify, provide a priori evidence. Because if there was any question, I was proof, wasn't I? Or was it the other way around, the charges against him now proof that something had happened to me?

This is all I could find: "It really bothers me to think about that girl . . . It's made me very upset. I really feel for her. For them. For . . . I wish I could help." My voice got wobbly.

It's so quiet even in my memory of this moment. I didn't want to make myself unpleasant. I didn't want to claim anything, accept any mantle. I didn't want to hurt my dad.

And here's the question I didn't ask, though it loomed in my mind: "Did you help take Toshi from his mother? Why did you do that? How?"

An image: a man's large hand around the slim wrist of a boy, a deed creating an irrevocable before and after.

Instead, I said, "Let me know the outcome."

I DON'T REMEMBER if he volunteered the information when he had it, or if my mom did, or if I had to ask for it, and if so, from whom. Somehow I learned the verdict. My cousin was found guilty of aggravated child assault and sent to prison for five years.

T oshi's tumultuous childhood was apparent to me during the earliest years of my own, and even before I learned how he was taken from his mother, I wondered how events in his own life affected his decision to come into my bedroom at night. It's hard to find firm answers. The taboo around sex with children makes pedophilia a difficult area of study. Those who have a sexual attraction to children—whether they've acted upon it or not—are reluctant to come forward voluntarily for evaluation. Researchers, always human, may find it particularly hard to separate their negative emotional responses from their investigation. But work has been done.

Psychologists often categorize pedophiles into two types. Fixated pedophiles are people who are sexually attracted only to children and not to adults. Regressed pedophiles are people who will engage in sex with children as well as with adults. Sometimes the sexual interest in a child arises for a regressed pedophile when there is no better option, and sometimes that interest is preferential. It may also be triggered by certain conditions, such as extreme stress.

There is no research that shows a history of sexual abuse results in pedophilia. Most pedophiles have no association with childhood and sexuality.

However, pedophilia, especially fixated pedophilia, often accompanies personality disorders such as thick-skinned narcissism and/or antisocial personality, and these personality disorders are most typically seen in people who have some kind of early childhood trauma. Some of this trauma might be sexual in nature, but sexual abuse alone suffered by children who otherwise grew up in nurturing households is not a significant contributing factor. Rather, it's children who were raised by an extremely neglectful primary caretaker, or who endured repeated physical beatings, or who were otherwise deprived of consistent affection and attention who may learn they must take from others to have important needs met. To an adult with a disordered personality, children are attractive as sexual objects because they are seen as weak and an easy source to take from.

Although most pedophiles were not themselves sexually abused, people who are sexually abused as children can form an association between childhood and sexuality, and if that association is created in the mind of a person who is also deeply narcissistic or anti-social, he or she might act upon these associations out of convenience or in an attempt to restore balance when feeling under stress or unfairly treated.

There's also some relatively new research suggesting that pedophilia has physiological roots. Pedophiles tend to be shorter than the average person, and to have a lower IQ. They're also more likely to be left-handed, and to have suffered head injuries before the age of thirteen. I haven't been able to find any literature that examines the link between head injuries and physical child abuse, but it's not a leap to expect battered children to have experienced higher incidents of blackouts and concussions than others. As with so many aspects of human tendency and behavior, nature and nurture are not easily untwined.

Whatever its roots, research suggests that an attraction to children is not something that can be fixed, or erased, at least not in adults. When it comes to preventing offense, there's been some success with treatment that encourages pedophiles to take responsibility for their actions, to identify and avoid triggers, and to identify and replace cognitive distortions. Prescribing testosterone-lowering medication to those who have repeatedly sexually abused children has also been shown to be effective. But neither of these methods have unambiguously impressive results, and it's rare for people to seek treatment before they've acted on their impulses and been caught. People with sexual thoughts about children are often in denial about it and about the impact of their actions. Also, the stigma against pedophiles, along with mandatory reporting statutes that require mental health professionals to report suspected child abuse, can keep people from seeking professional help to control their attractions or to address the depression and other mental health problems that might stem from it.

It was not an easy decision for me to write about my sexual abuse by a family member, knowing as I do that my story—like all stories—involves the lives of people who deserve privacy. One guideline I gave myself was to stick to my own thoughts and feelings as much as possible, and when it came to other people, to recount only what I experienced or what an observer could notice, rather than try to psychoanalyze or pry beneath the surface. I wasn't a witness to Toshi's early years. In any case, dwelling on them might give the impression that I'm making excuses for him. There is no excuse for emotionally, physically, or sexually abusing a child. But what becomes clear with study is that childhood trauma often begets trauma for the next generation of children. People who commit horrific acts are also fellow humans and were once children. The lack of a clear program of rehabilitation for pedophilia is one of the things that makes the issue of child sexual abuse so messy, uncomfortable, and depressing.

I have more or less come of age with the modern American awareness of childhood sex abuse. When second-wave feminists started discussing the issue in the 1960s, there was little public acknowledgement of the topic. Though laws were starting to change to reflect a more emphatic understanding of sexual assault as a crime, by the time I was born in 1968, it'd only been about a year since all states required physicians suspecting abuse to report it. Barring dramatic injury to the genitals, the suspicion probably wouldn't even have arisen terribly often. The warning signs of sex abuse had not been systematically identified and they were not commonly disseminated to doctors, school administrators, clergy, or family members. The teacher that girls knew not to visit alone or the uncle you tried to squirm away from before he could pull you to his lap weren't necessarily viewed as part of a larger problem. Creepy people were to be avoided, but whatever happened at their hand was not something that necessarily needed to be discussed.

Information became more available in the 1970s. In 1974, the year after my own abuse ended, Congress passed the Child Abuse Prevention and Treatment Act, dedicated to identifying, preventing, and treating child abuse, including sexual abuse, by providing funding to the states for all these things. In subsequent years, knowledge was collected and expounded upon. Child sex abuse, pedophilia, and incest emerged as psychiatric specialties. Advocates of child victims organized. In 1979, the National Abuse Coalition was created in order to pressure Congress to create more laws specifically around the area of sexual abuse.

In the 1980s, the topic exploded. At the dawn of the decade, when Heather Moosier and I began walking to our music lessons together to the soundtrack of her stories of sex, *Michelle Remembers* was published. The book, an account of satanic ritual abuse—including sex abuse—initiated what has since been called a moral panic, but at the time looked like the unveiling of a ubiquitous, unsavory truth: depravity was everywhere, and innocence would be preyed upon. Overlapping the conversation about ritual abuse and the issue of repressed memory were the conversations about the recovery process of victims of incest and pedophilia. Writing one's story was considered an important part of healing, a practice dramatized in *The Color Purple*, which won the Pulitzer in 1983, and recommended by *The Courage to Heal: A Guide for Women Survivors of Child Sexual Abuse*.

But critics of this new movement came out loudly, too, underscoring that the authors of *The Courage to Heal* lacked a background in psychiatry and accusing them of sowing seeds of interfamily conflict where none needed to exist. Just because someone *felt* they had been abused did not mean they *had* been abused, skeptics posited. And even if molestation *had* taken place, it was being overused as an excuse, offered as an explanation for any grievance, an escape from adult responsibility. In 1995, Katie Roiphe published "Making the Incest Scene," an essay in *Harper's* that catalogued a long list of the recent novels that had used incest as a salacious and oversimplified plot device. Roiphe declared the topic overdone and boring.

The growing backlash did not affect the trend toward legislation that made sex abuse easier to prosecute, however, and throughout the 1980s and 1990s, almost all states enacted laws that extended the statute of limitations for child sex crimes, recognizing the unique circumstances surrounding a violation perpetuated on a child. The states handle the details of the extended statues in various ways. On the one extreme is Alabama, one of the few states that still maintains no special statute of limitations for child sex crimes at all. The charges must be brought within two years of date of injury. If you were abused when you were five, you need to report it before you turn eight to have any hope of redress. On the other extreme is Alaska, where a statute provides that a person may bring action for the felony sexual abuse of a minor at any time. Presumably, a fifty-five-year-old woman could bring charges against her seventy-five-year-old father.

But most states established an outer limit for reporting and pressing charges against such a crime. Some states work from the age of majority—they extend the statute of limitations five, ten, or twenty years past the age of eighteen. Other states focus more on the date of discovery—you must take action within a set number of years from realizing the abuse occurred and/or identifying the injuries it caused. Or the statutes combine these two things: considering the age of majority alongside the reason for discovery of injury.

UPON LEARNING that my cousin was on trial for the sexual assault of a child, and with only the most confused understanding of how the criminal justice system works, I convinced myself that the most honorable action for me would be to seek legal recognition of my own molestation and prevent the current charges from existing in a vacuum. In other words, to come forward. But in Pennsylvania, the law is straightforward, and it precluded this. The statue of limitations is extended twelve years from the date of the minor victim's reaching his or her age of majority. After thirty, the victim loses the right to press charges.

I was thirty-three when my cousin stood trial—disempowered in this regard, but also off the hook. Though I felt it to be the responsible thing to do, the thought of seeking restitution for this long-ago crime terrified me to my core. I was relieved I could avoid it.

The New Mexico statute is more nuanced. It states, "Legal action must be initiated by the victim's twenty-fourth birthday, or three years from the date of discovery of abuse, or from the date the victim had reason to know of the childhood sexual abuse and that the abuse resulted in injury." This seemed to leave me neither clearly absolved from taking action nor in a reasonable position from which to do so. Instead, the language of the statute invited me

214 / ZOE ZOLBROD

to respond as I usually did when given cause to reflect on what happened between Toshi and me: I stumbled through a field of questions, defensiveness,
and confusion. I wasn't clear what would constitute a "reason to know" of
abuse. What if one had a "reason to know" but not proof of resulting injury? Are the abuse and injury so indelibly tied that if the latter doesn't exist,
neither does the former? The way the statute read made it seem like I would
have had to go to therapy and get diagnosed with psychological problems
in order to have been a victim of a crime. If I hadn't felt the need to do so,
was that one more piece of evidence suggesting that what Toshi did to me
was not that bad? I hated the way my psychology had to be dragged into the
justice system.

YET I UNDERSTOOD why it had come to be. The emphasis on psychological
injury is important not just in order to understand and treat it, but also to
counter the widespread cultural—near universal—expectation that vulnerable bodies will be used sexually, that it's a matter of course, to be shrugged
off and moved on from unless physical injury is dramatically present.

Here's why it matters, the victim's advocates must state, again and again,
so we listen: why it matters is the long-term effect. It's not just a child's body
we're talking about—not just a half-formed consciousness that might not
even remember how it was used, or, in the case of post-pubescent minors,
a sexually mature pleasure seeker who might even enjoy aspects of the encounter—it's cause for a damaged adult, too. People make so many claims of
concern for children, but we blur our eyes at them when it's too hard to see.
It's the maladjusted grown-ups with still sore wounds, those who can speak
for themselves, who command attention. Who get laws changed.

And, in some cases, who perpetuate damage.

I want to be an advocate for children and others whose bodies are invad-
ed, who become occupied territories that the spirit evacuates or that guerril-
la armies rise up to fight. I want to get laws changed, the world changed, to
better protect the sexually vulnerable. I'm so grateful to the people who have
done this work, who do it every day.

But to the very marrow of my bones, where there's an ache for it, I seem
to want control of the essential, mysterious heart of my own experience, and

turning to either psychology or a court threatened to cede that control. Coming into my own sexual maturity during the years when the battle to define the meaning of child sexual abuse was playing out like a melodrama—a clash of the titans between those who believed that sexual abuse is commonplace, traumatic, and character-shaping or those who see such claims as manipulative fabrications—I could not find a place for myself. My small, large, strange deck of memories didn't fit in either hand. I didn't want to put my cards down to be played. Perhaps if I'd had, they could have been of use in the trial against Toshi. The need for me to keep my story close is part of what plagues me with guilt.

I know. I know. I know. It's not my fault. None of it is my fault.

But what would have happened if I had told?

MY FATHER USED TO put my brother and me to sleep. He'd sit at the child's table that was placed between our two beds and sing us song after song—lullabies giving way to popular tunes from the forties giving way to Army songs, drawing on every chorus he knew on the many nights when I had trouble letting go of consciousness. I'm not sure whether he started doing this at the age when the abuse occurred, but let me say he had. Let me imagine that one evening, in between the fifth and sixth song, with my brother's breathing already deep and steady, and my father expressing wonderment—never impatience, as I remember it—that I remained so alert, I would have said, "Toshi comes in the room sometimes after you leave and wants to touch me under my underpants."

I have a notion of myself at that age as something between a spy and a prisoner who exhibited model behavior while sharpening a shiv—taking in more than I gave out, omniscient but constrained, suspicious, plotting. My father might have said some right things: That it shouldn't have happened. That he was going to make sure it didn't happen again. That I had done the right thing by telling him. When my father eventually left my bedroom, my words would have spread throughout the rest of the house. Other people would have been told. And I would have felt more naked than before.

I could have told my mom. On the day in New Mexico when I was sick and she came in from the outing with my dad and brother to feel my head, when she asked whether Toshi had given me my medicine, I could have said, "Toshi didn't give me medicine and he got in bed with me and pulled his pants down and I didn't like it." She may have responded tenderly, but more likely the news would have set off a manic alarm. She might have cried *"WHAT?"* in a voice that rang with accusation, with her teeth bared, her neck taut. "What do you mean he pulled his pants down? Are you sure? Why would he *do* that?" I would have lay on that sick bed, pinned again, this time by questions and a different kind of fear that my words would cause a long-lasting trouble, that Toshi would be called to account.

Why is that? Why would a confrontation with Toshi in the presence of my parents have been so unthinkable? And here I'm forced to acknowledge the way I conform to the basic child sexual abuse victim template: there had been a bond between us, between Toshi and me, however queasy and uneasy, and telling either parent would have taken a cleaver to it. Having to face him would have meant having to stare at the blood, be seen with the hatchet in my own hand.

Didn't I want that? Don't I sometimes have violent fantasies about offenders?

Yes, I do now, but not back then, and these fantasies are about fantasy offenders, or offenders of others, not my own.

In any case, let me imagine that I had told my parents, let me avert my eyes from the blood. What would have happened next? Toshi probably would have been shipped off sooner to the same place he ended up anyway, the ju- venile detention home on the outskirts of town, this time labeled as a sex of- fender. There exists some evidence that if pedophiliac tendencies are caught early, there's greater hope of averting enactment of them. But it was 1973. That evidence didn't exist yet, nor did the treatments. The field is still consid- ered new today. There would have been no reliable help for him.

Or for me. I, too, might have been sent to some kind of counselor. The treatment of child sex abuse victims was also in its infancy, but even if there'd been a local expert, I can picture how stiffly and sullenly I might have pre- sented myself to a psychologist, how alienating I likely would have found the encounters. Given my desire to interpret my life for myself, I don't regret not going.

So, WHAT IF I would have waited until I was an adult? What would have happened if I or either of my parents—my father, it would have had to have been—had urged some more definitive action in the face of my mid-twenties announcement that this abuse had occurred? Perhaps he could have created a forum for some sort of restorative justice.

In my case, in the 1990s my family was all spread out. No two of us in the relevant quartet—cousin, mother, father, me—lived in the same state. I hadn't seen Toshi in five years. But imagine if a rendezvous could have been possible. My throat constricts at the thought of it. Would I have been able to speak? To say something like: "You molested me starting when I was four years old. It's been a stone in my shoe all these years. I think you owe me an apology. Please don't do it again."

If he had looked at me and said "I'm sorry," instinctively, I might have said, "That's okay." And I imagine I might have felt something lifting.

But even in my imaginings, it's hard to believe a request from me would have made him keep his hands to himself, his mouth above board, his dick in his pants.

What might have given him the ability to have stopped with me? What if I'd have pressed charges in my twenties, when many changes to the legal system had been made and I was still young enough to fit inside the statute of limitations? We're just imagining, here, let's not get bogged down with the scant evidence of the crime, the logistical difficulty, the financial drain, the emotional toll on myself and my family. Let's just pretend I did it and I won. Then he would have had to don the label of child sex offender a handful of years earlier. Might this notice to family, friends, neighbors, potential employers, and the public at large have spared someone from him, have spared him from himself? Maybe.

The year I told my parents that Toshi had molested me was the same year Congress passed the Sexual Offender Act of 1994, commonly referred to as Megan's Law, because it was created in response to the murder of seven-year-old Megan Kanka by a convicted sex offender who lived across the street from her. The law mandates harsh sentencing for repeat offenders and requires that states share with the public information about anyone who has been convicted of felony sex assault—often including the offender's residential address, photograph, and crime along with their name. Internet usage has become ubiquitous in the years since the law's passage, and today, information about offenders is almost as easy to obtain as the weather forecast or yesterday's sport's scores. One consequence is that the men can be publically harassed and pressured to leave their communities.

Another consequence is that people who are made particularly uneasy by the existence of sex offenders can stoke their anxiety. I've gone through periods where I've sought these registries out, stared at the photos lined up in rows, squinted into the eyes of these men—the ones who live in my community, the one who is related to me. His hair is more gray now than black, and two deep lines are drawn down from his cheekbones to his jaw, but he's trim, his face is not sagging or swollen, like so many of the others. He's recognizable to me as the strange, taciturn, handsome hippie boy whose stride through the dining room could rattle the plates in the built-in cabinets while I sat in the adjoining room playing with my plastic animals or my brother's army men. He was my family member, my father's charge. What righteous certitude I would have had to muster to press the issue, what conviction that the court-defined punishment would match and not supersede the crime. What proof of injury I would have had to display. I didn't have any of those things.

It feels self-important—and I know it's inaccurate—to lump myself in with the many now-infamous people on sports staffs and school administrations and in the Catholic hierarchy who have turned away uncomfortably from glanced, sensed, intimated, complicated suggestions and blunt accusations that children are being sexually abused within their esteemed institutions. But though reading about instances where child sexual assault is downplayed can make me so angry I breathe in a pant, I also understand how it happens. When something is both horrible and commonplace, especially when it's caught in the web of loyalty and blood, it's easy to look away, make the bet that it won't happen again, assume if it's really of great consequence, someone else will force it to stop.

In 2008, a study conducted in New Jersey concluded that Megan's Law has not been effective in preventing repeat offenses or reducing the number of child sex assault victims in that state. Critics have noted that among the law's inadvertent adverse effects is the difficulty it can create for the victims. Since so many offenders are convicted for crimes against a family member, and since they often return to the family's home or proximity when released, the attention they garner when their residence and crimes are made public affects the whole clan, makes it difficult to move on. But the law, though expensive to implement, is politically popular. It's a definitive sign that society doesn't tolerate child sexual abuse, a distraction from the reality that, despite the near hysteria over the issue, so many of us—perpetrators, protectors, victims, witnesses or potential ones—are bumbling through a fog when we confront the issue under our own noses, under our own covers, stuffed under our beds.

I n my hometown, ninth graders still attended the junior high, but despite being stuck in the same old building with the younger kids, by the time my friends and I had reached that grade, we'd graduated from the world of basement make-out parties to going on dates in cars. It was traditional for high school boys to recruit girlfriends from the exiled freshmen class, compensating for the indignity they'd had to face when the girls in their own grade started dating up, and by Christmas of my freshman year, I had settled on a popular junior. Some of his friends were going out with some of mine, and between them they had access to cars, legal-aged brothers who would come through with alcohol when the fake IDs failed, and, on many weekends, empty homes for us to go to. Instead of smuggling a few beers from our parents' fridges or pouring off some of their gin into jelly jars, my friends and I now partied with cases of Genny Cream Ale and bottles of Jack. Instead of kissing and groping on a floor in a room full of others, we now retreated to beds or couches in rooms that had doors on them. Intoxicated as much by the smell of Jovan Musk and the feel of skin on skin as by the booze, we proceeded to very heavy petting, pairing off into the bedrooms of houses where the single mom was working the nightshift or the parents had gone for the weekend. Eventually we'd reconvene as a same-sex cell, usually at a sleepover at Susie Tyson's house, where we'd chart how far we'd gone, make bawdy and insinuating jokes about how much we'd liked it or they had, and ponder what we were willing to do next.

By some measures, fourteen seems young to be doing these things, drinking regularly and dating so steadily for the purpose of sexual exploration. We were still kid-like in many ways, mouthy and gaggle-minded as middle schoolers are, and when neighbors saw us trip into the cars of muscle-pumped guys who shaved, it must have looked dubious to some. But I perceive a great benefit to having moved further along the highway of adolescence while still in such tight tandem with a group of friends, at least given how the stars were aligned in my particular constellation. Toward the end of high school, relationships start to become more singular, focused on pairs of friends or romantic couples that don't fit as neatly into a pack and so allow for some privacy, which can feel blessed by that point, I know. But in my clique the plurality of the early teen years encouraged—even forced—an openness about our sexuality that was the opposite of the night-black loneliness I bore in the wake of the secret games Toshi imposed on me ten years earlier.

My friends and I all knew which part of whose bodies had been touched and gazed upon by our boyfriends, what tickled or hurt or felt good, what we'd touched in turn and how we felt about it, what scared us. Of course, all this sharing could have been used as ammunition by friends that were not really, or who were far enough apart on the spectrum of experience or opportunity to be threatened by the difference—it happens all the time, to dreadful effect. But that wasn't the case in our group. I recall that mostly we helped each other; I don't remember much shaming, pressure, or judgment. As far as I know, none of us slipped off with another's boyfriend, but we multiplied our knowledge of the species by each sharing what we knew and liked and didn't like about our own. Oh, how we'd smirk and squeal when Marvin Gaye's "Sexual Healing" would come on the radio. How we'd groan and clutch ourselves as we listened to Prince albums and counted down the days until Ryan Earl's parents left to visit his sister at college, leaving him alone in the house. Going off to meet a boy in an adult-empty duplex would have been much less fun and more frightening if we had done it on our own. We were lucky in each other.

We were also lucky in the quality of that first round of boys, too, with whom we stayed until they approached graduation. Most of them had managed an act of intercourse before we came along, but not from a regular squeeze, and they were respectful of our lesser experience. Soon enough they said they loved us, but they never used this declaration to plead or to pressure. While on the one hand, the age difference between the girls and the boys—two years a great many back then—might have accelerated the pace of my friends' and my experimentation, it also worked as a safeguard, gave us an excuse to hold back when we wanted to, gave the boys an excuse to slow down, too, to be protective. I enjoyed playing the neophyte. I enjoyed the way my boyfriend Ronnie slowly stoked then rode the wave of my desire without getting too far in front of it. I felt him attuned to me. It was nothing like the wrestler and his octopus hands.

There was communication and negotiation within each dyad, and it existed in partnership with that carried out by the larger group. For one thing, since we all knew what each other were doing, when coupled up boy-girl we could talk about our friends' progress and use it as a way to talk about our own. The back-and-forth with my friends, and their back-and-forth with their boyfriends, and the boys' back-and-forth with each other all helped to keep the base-running moving forward at the right pace. For example: as had been the case when we were just starting to make out, I was not the quickest in our group to reach sexual milestones, and it took me longer than many of my friends to want to see a penis or touch one, to take the first steps towards a hand-job. I'd rolled around for hours near-naked with my boyfriend, but he'd always kept his pants on. When I felt ready to put my hand down his jeans—or almost ready, ready as I thought I'd ever be—the communication passed along through the grapevine, from Reba, to her boyfriend, to mine. By the time Saturday night rolled around, all six or eight of us who packed into one car for the drive to the evening's vacant house knew that my boyfriend and I were going to cross a threshold, and so when the time came to divvy up into the two beds and one couch, he and I were granted a prime spot—the master bedroom.

The house, off a dark and unfamiliar road, wasn't one of our usuals, and I'm not sure I ever knew the connection that brought us there. It was likely shady. Maybe a teammate who'd graduated a couple years ago was now having sex with an older woman, or a key had been slipped to someone in return for a favor that didn't bear scrutiny. As the younger ones along for the ride, my friends and I didn't ask questions, we just filed in. Someone turned on the light and the radio and the heat. There was spongy shag carpeting and wood paneling, and the pine cone air freshener didn't quite cover up the smell of stale cigarette smoke and mold. But the boys had been planning ahead; the refrigerator was already full of Old Milwaukee. After one tallboy, my discomfort at being at a stranger's sagging house melted away. I'd guess I was on my third can when my boyfriend invited me to go into the bedroom. It was right off the living room, and it had a flimsy pocket door. I backed into the big bed and fell down on it. I turned my head to one side and noticed the open closet, the pile of women's shoes within, a toppled pump with a stained insole. The room was not quite spinning, but I was deliciously drunk. Ronnie wrestled with the sliding door, lifting it off the carpet to get it shut all the way. When closed, it was outlined by a string of golden light, the room's only illumination. Then he was beside me, and we were kissing, grinding, rolling hips. "Baby Come to Me," was on the radio—not a dance song, but it became one, the rhythm a revelation as we hula-ed within it. Pleasure. Pleasure. Pleasure. My blouse and front-clasp bra had fallen open, but this had gotten de rigueur. The energy was all in our hips. I squeezed my hand into the press of them and tentatively skid its heel up and down the rigid core at the crotch of Ronnie's Levis. I'd done that before, but this time on my third or fourth upstroke, he sucked in his stomach and steered my hand up further and then under his waistband, where my fingertips immediately glanced the head of his hard dick, almost peeking out. He wasn't wearing underwear; he'd come prepared.

The nervousness I'd been feeling about this introduction dropped away. It felt nice! A skein of silk dusted in powder. My fingers sparked as they touched it, relayed a yes. He plunged my hand down further, and I took hold of the shaft. My grip felt just right. After a couple guided demonstrations, my confidence grew and I took over the pulling. There was nothing gross or awkward about it. Nothing at all. In fact, it felt natural. It felt right. I *liked* it.

I got my hips back into motion. I swung my pelvis lustily. I'd been known for my dirty dancing moves since I was eight or nine, and now it all fit together in the rhythm.

I don't remember if he came that night. I don't remember how we stopped, what happened next. I was lost in the moment. I've mostly stayed there, in a way—my body grooving, cock in hand, the sense of nice-to-meet-you. Happiness unclouded by my too-early introduction to sex and penises. In the glide up and down of this straight and solid one, in our friendliness with each other, something became clear to me: that was not this.

Ronnie and I were together a long time. He was horny but considerate. Doing what I wanted to do with him did not create an assumption that we'd keep ratcheting things up beyond my point of comfort. I never gave me him a blow job, we never went all the way. He never pressured me. Fundamentally, he was a nice boy.

And so was the next one, and the next. I was lucky. But maybe not just that. Even the ones who couldn't easily be called nice I chose for a reason. I could choose now. I'd learned how to pick them.

D on't get excited. It's anticlimactic. When my son was in his last year of preschool, my employer offered a new life-balance program that covered a set number of visits to a list of pre-approved counselors. My husband and I were having a hard time making a decision about whether to have another child, and I convinced him that talking to a third party might help us sort through our issues. It wasn't as if one of us knew we wanted a second baby and the other did not; we were both caught in a tangle of desire and ambivalence knotted around conflicts of time, money, roles, and career and creative ambitions.

Because it was my idea to talk to someone, the therapist suggested I come in to meet her alone before bringing my husband. Her home office turned out to be in the same area in which Anthony and I were looking to buy a house—in fact, we had viewed a couple right across the street, and the grievously high price of them and their ilk was one of the things that was making us question the cost, financially and emotionally, of expanding our family.

The therapist and I made small talk about real estate while she did her paperwork, and then she asked me to sketch out the basics of myself and my upbringing: what did mine and Anthony's configuration look like? What had been the configuration of my family of origin, and how did I feel about that? I answered by telling who worked in what capacity, how hard and how happily. We lingered for awhile on the dynamic between my parents, the constant thrum of dissatisfaction and financial anxiety buzzing from my mother, my father's cheerful but intense dedication to his modestly paid career and to us. We discussed my late-breaking understanding of how hard my mother had worked and how much she had dedicated, too. She'd been active with us and at our schools; she'd borne the burden when we took in family members, first my father's teenaged nephew, then my mother's dad.

And then, without thinking, I said, "Starting when I was four I was molested for about a year by the nephew, my cousin. I don't think it had much of an effect on me, but it just seems like something I should say when we're talking about this stuff." It'd been four years since I'd learned about the charges against my cousin and my dad's role in his disrupted childhood, but I didn't mention these more recent complexities.

She blinked behind her glasses, rims the same silver-gold color of her short hair, lenses that needed cleaning. "I'm sorry to hear that," she said gently. "If you think it didn't have much effect on you, you're probably right."

So much for my fears that psychologists tended to see sexual molestation as the cause of any problem, which were stoked by the once widespread accusations that they pushed people to dredge up memories that weren't even quite there. The therapist's response was nothing like what I had feared all these years, which was that the sentences would be met with the leash-pulling certitude of a dog sniffing for a bone, with the imposition of a story that I didn't recognize as my own. Trends in psychology must have changed since the eighties and nineties, the information about child sex abuse no longer unfolding and new. Yet I felt let down. In some ways, I suppose I was still looking for what I also had never wanted: a grown-up to take this tangled mass of yarn from my too-small hands, give it back to me balled up and explained, categorized if not taken care of. But I looked no further for a therapist who might have been able to help me understand this yearning. That kind of assistance was not to be.

After the appointment I walked back to my office in the yellow glare of midday September. When I passed a little house with a newly planted FOR SALE sign, I took the time to survey the exterior. It looked small and plain, possibly affordable, but also solid, suitable to our needs. I called the listing agent immediately. The house was above our price range, but not by so very much. After we viewed it, we saw that it needed to be rehabbed to be livable, but that the bones were good. We waited until the price went down and then we made an offer.

During this process, Anthony and I visited the therapist together a few times to talk through the question of baby-making and all its attendant issues. But ultimately our ability to buy and remodel the house had a far greater effect on our decision about whether and when to have a second child than anything said in her office.

WORRYING ABOUT the cost of a bigger home and how to pay for it explained only part of my ambivalence about having a second child. I was also tormented by my inability to maintain my creative writing life while working and parenting the kid I already had. When three women I had been on a writing residency with seven years before arranged to meet in Minnesota for a reunion writing retreat, I felt almost embarrassed to go, so bereft of a project did I feel, so alienated from my identity as a writer. I also felt terrified—what did my writer self have to say after being ignored for so long? I wasn't sure I wanted to hear it.

Despite my misgivings I packed up my notebooks and made the trip to Duluth, which was close to the place we had all met. It was early May when I went, but that far north, the spring thaw still felt raw. In shady spots, the ice-covered ground creaked and cracked when stepped on. Trickles of cold water dripped between the jutting rocks, shaping the earth incrementally. Though the presence of the other women was a salve to me—each one of us occupied a different decade and a different stage of parenting and writing life—I kept largely to myself. I wrote in my notebooks some, but mostly I read through them, sitting outside as much as possible, chasing the sun by using as a desk one then another of the rough picnic tables that dotted the off-season resort where we were lodged together in a suite.

What my spiral-bounds were revealing to me was that I'd written more than I gave myself credit for in the past few years. The scribbled longhand notes were a cross between the journaling I did in my twenties and the scene-making I'd segued into from that. Whether fiction or nonfiction, the subject was very often sex and issues related to the abuse—Toshi, my father's history with him, the mysteries of the past I'd been tied to since before I was born.

In between notebooking, I walked the rocky shore of crashing, gray Lake Superior, tossing pebbles into the waves, taking in the noise and vastness and my solitude. My movement released something in me that my pen-moving had begun already to pry at. I progressed from pebbles to heaving large stones toward the waves, grunting from the effort, then hollering, yelling out realizations and snippets of quotations. I got stuck on the last phrase from *The Great Gatsby*—"borne back ceaselessly into the past"—and repeated it while crying, until my face was covered in tears and snot, my fleece sleeve stiff with wiping at it. I walked some more, noticing the clutch of feathers poking from a decomposing gull, the glitter in a stone cracked in half, the artful rock tower left behind by a previous sojourner.

On the last night I decamped to the property's lodge, a space with foosball tables, worn couches, and shelves full of the wavy crossword puzzles and board games waiting for vacationing families. But this week those in our party were the only guests, and I took over the main table, spread out my beer and snacks and notebooks, and wrote compulsively for hours. My past was my subject, and I knew that when I went home to our new house I was going to find a way to write seriously again.

I GOT PREGNANT a couple months after I returned from Duluth, but I maintained my commitment. At first I tried to fictionalize the material, but I found that wasn't freeing me from my confusion and shame and fear about the topic of childhood sexual abuse. In fact, writing fiction left me feeling like I was sneaking around, in some way revisiting the slippery, sly pursuits and evasions of my early youth—the bed creaking and Toshi whispering; the fantasy life I developed for myself, which sometimes permeated my reality in a way my playmates could not have known but were implicated in; the sense of hiding something and not being sure of what it was.

My most electric writing occurred when I grappled directly with my own memories. My most clearheaded responses were to current events that raised issues of sexual abuse that resonated with my own past. I began swelling with the feeling that my own story was the one I wanted to tell. Anthony supported me in this, even when my excavations into territory I had avoided all my life made me moody and tense, and even though he found it too painful to read what I was producing. His response contributed to a question I already had: for both myself and others, would my telling this story be more likely to heal, or help, or hurt? And what about the fact that I'd have to talk to my dad?

J

ust the thought of my father makes me feel better about the world. How can I describe him? For all the declarations about him I've made in this book, I don't think I have yet.

He appreciates music, all kinds. I was mostly unmoved by the symphonies that played often in our kitchen, but I was influenced by the other stuff he listened to—bluegrass, Beatles, folk. And when I started discovering music of my own beyond Top 40, he was eager to hear what I gravitated to, gave it serious attention. Together in the car, around town, and then on road trips we took together when I was in college, we'd listen to Kate Bush, Laurie Anderson, The Smiths, New Order by way of Joy Division, and he'd sometimes listen alone to them, too. We'd discuss the lyrics and tone, and his superior sense of musical form could help me hear things anew. We'd also listen to singer-songwriters he liked. Nanci Griffith was a favorite. When "There's a Light Beyond These Woods (Mary Margaret)" came on, about two friends who grow up in a small town and dream of the day they'll "move to New York City and drink the poet's wine," he'd often say, "This song always reminds me of you and Reba." It made me happy—the pretty, wistful, slightly sappy song

I wouldn't otherwise have given myself permission to listen to at that time of being too-cool-for-school; the reminder of me and Reba as girls; the pleasure of being seen as an emerging adult but remembered as a child.

But that's a digression, just a sweet memory of the comfort newly adult children are apt to derive from a certain kind of non-controlling parent. Here's what I see as especially telling: several years ago, on one of his visits to our family, my dad came down to my office to take me to lunch. Over our meal, he told me that he's always disliked rap music, so much so that he couldn't even listen to it, and that this has bothered him, since some of his students liked it, and surely it must have something to offer. He wanted to understand what. So he decided to turn it on while he was in the shower, when he couldn't get out and change the station.

"And you know what?," he said with wonder. "As I listened I realized something. It's warrior music. It's about vanquishing foes, developing reputation. It comes from a lineage that includes Beowulf and Gilgamesh." He said he understood its merits, even if he still didn't choose to listen to it.

HE CAME TO VISIT me in Chicago soon after I'd moved there. I'd been in the city only a few months, but I'd already learned to inure myself to street people. It was a pose to appear city-savvy enough not to care, and a protection against over-empathy and despair, as well as against intrusions that could turn threatening. I was proud of it. My dad and I were sitting near the railing of an outdoor café on the Gold Coast when a panhandler approached and asked to be helped out. He didn't bother to soften his aspect, which was rough and prickling with angry need, and I wanted my father to ignore him, erect the frost barrier that I employed often in public. Instead, my dad addressed the man civilly, reached into his own pocket, and then poured into the man's palm a good handful of silver. The panhandler looked at it, disgusted.

"Man, don't you have any bills?" he said.

"Hey, I'm on a budget too!" my father responded.

The incident made me laugh for years. Where I saw the approach of a booze-smelling, red-eyed menace toward a too-well-meaning small town naïf, my father saw an exchange between two people on budgets—one who'd run short, and one with enough excess to take his daughter out to a leisurely lunch, but basically equal.

The rudeness shown to him by the Chicago panhandler didn't sour my father. Of course it didn't—it wouldn't have been the first time his kindness was met with scorn. Although I have at times been irritated by his insistence on looking on the bright side of any situation, my dad doesn't turn away from elemental human need the way I can. He recently recounted to me a story about an Albuquerque homeless man who he frequently sees at a certain busy intersection. Sometimes my dad would roll down his window to give the man a couple bucks. After one such exchange, he'd gotten to thinking about what it'd be like to be in the man's place, wondering what a person in those straits did when he wasn't lacing through cars in the quiver of their exhaust. Does he even have anything to read? my dad thought, considering where he himself would look for solace if he were on the streets. So my dad put some old magazines into his car and the next time he saw the man, he gave him a dollar and asked him if he'd by any chance like some reading material. The man's face lit up. "Yes!" he said. "One of the worst things about my situation is I just get so bored. God bless you!" So each week after he was done with them, my father would take his *New Yorkers* and *Nations* to his vehicle and keep them there until he crossed paths with the man.

I would not be surprised if my dad slipped in some copies of poems amidst the magazines and dollar bills, too. He believes that Wordsworth can speak to anyone who takes the time to listen, that we still have a lot to learn from Longfellow. He offers these poets to his students on the Navajo reservation, building a case for them by connecting their work to Navajo cosmology. In a world where writers like my friends and me look outward on a daily basis to see how to magnify our own voices, he continues to drive up to a remote corner of the reservation where his cell phone is out of range, to teach Composition and English 101. He spends a night on a cot in the library there so he can get two days in. Over the years, he's painstakingly fine-tuned a curriculum for this particular group of students—adults of various ages from a high desert tribal culture who have grown up far away from mainstream America and who have their own way of learning. He's particularly excited about illuminating the way sentences make meaning by describing them in terms of the relationships most important in that community: subject and verb come together like a man and a woman, and their clauses are their living offspring. A compound sentence shows ties of extended kinship, and a paragraph is a clan. He sees in the system of the English language the most elemental connectedness. I couldn't care less about teaching subject-verb agreement, until I hear him talk about it. Even then, my interest is in his enthusiasm, not in predication. Something about my father makes me feel happy and clean and interesting—as if I'm an improved person by proxy. It's an important feeling for me, a part of my identity since I was small.

I HAVE NEVER GONE through a stage when I was more critical of my father than grateful for him, but there were years when I saw his cheerfulness toward any stranger mostly as a bastion of male privilege. For me, as for most women, especially when we're young, encounters with random people who approach on the street can often turn gendered and sexual. On numerous occasions I've seen a panhandler's demeanor transform from ingratiating, "Spare some change, miss?" to enraged, "Bitch! Suck my dick then!" During my early days in the city, an unkempt man said hello to me as we stepped on the train one evening, and I returned the greeting perceptibly enough so as not to be accused of rudeness, but primly enough, I thought, to foreclose further contact, and then looked up from my book a few minutes later to see him standing across from me and jerking off while licking his lips and staring into my face. Every pleasantry had the potential to lead to its opposite.

The flip side of this kind of victimization was that when I was with a man, I disappeared in the presence of street people; my participation was not required at all. The beggar who approached my father and me at the café table didn't even look my way. Neither did the handfuls of twitchy or lurching or slurring men who'd approached various boyfriends and me at park benches or train platforms or bus shelters over the years. It was the guy to whom they'd direct their entreaties and diatribes, even as my presence sometimes complicated the dynamic between the two males: I was the audience for my guy to perform for, or the object leveraged for a payoff, and I would sense how I played into the calculations involved on both sides.

THE DYNAMIC DEMANDING that a woman needs a man to protect her from men remains commonplace all over the world. The message is communicated both implicitly and explicitly, in literature, tradition, advice, and the law. When and where I grew up, big brothers and especially fathers delivered it. The warnings to girls: "Don't go there. Don't do that. You can't trust him." The promises and threats: "If he hurts you, I'll kill him." "If you hurt her, I'll kill you." But my father, bucking convention, didn't participate in these rituals of concern. He never suggested I should be afraid or that I should circumscribe my movements in accordance with my gender. He did not look askance at any of the boys or men I had contact with. He did not see me as walking prey. I appreciated this even before I knew much about feminism. It fostered my independence. It helped me see myself as a person first.

But the expectation that a girl should have a male protector, with the father as the prototype for this role, is a deep one, and not without psychological consequence. There's a universal understanding that protection equals love, that a father should guard his daughter, become enraged when he cannot, has failed if he participates in any way in the trespass of her innocence. From the perspective of both the child I was and of the parent I now am, I find these assumptions heavy and limiting. I want to move beyond them. And yet there's a loneliness that sets in when I decamp from the ancient settlement, and I carry with me a nagging doubt: *should* my father have protected me better? Could he have? When I consider what happened to Toshi and to me and to at least one other girl, the expectations of protectorship point toward some blame of him. But this equation doesn't ring true to me. I don't accept it.

MY DAD'S INTEREST in others and his generosity of spirit makes him a good grandfather. It's such a pleasure to watch him light up for my children, and they for him. He has great difficulty walking now, but I've seen him gamely try to fit his way into the plastic tube on the slide in order to yodel up a silly message, or loll on a futon on the floor calling rhyming nonsense into a metal can, extending the joke elaborately and increasing the children's giggles to hilarity where I would have grown almost immediately weary. Some grandparents who go that far can't come back; they become heedless kids themselves again, not only spoiling the children indulgently but egging them on until their behavior gets out of control. But when I call that it's time for dinner or for bed, my father will turn on a dime and kindly say: "Oh, you've got to listen to your mom now."

I wonder how he learned the tricks of good grandparenting. He had no models. His had not played a strong role in his life—one was shot and killed in Poland before he was born, two were gassed in concentration camps, one was demolished by dislocation and poverty. His own parents mostly ignored my brother and me, or scolded us harshly, judged. I have one memory of being alone with my paternal grandfather, a short, clean-shaven, thick-spectacled man. Neither of us knew quite what to say when we found ourselves on the sun porch together. "What's the capital of Pennsylvania?" he asked me. I couldn't answer.

"You should know," he said. "You should know, know, know, know." The joints of his index finger were jagged, and he pointed at me with each repeated word.

Like my father, my grandfather was bent and hobbled by arthritis. I already show the signs in my feet and knees. But not everything is hereditary, passed down through the blood. Not everything is dependent on nurturing, either. Viewed in the context of his family, my father proves that many traits are concocted anew.

I so often feel a drudgery about family life. My father helps me see beyond it. My kids and my husband and I all bond around our fondness for him. My brother and my niece are put into a good mood by him, too. The seven of us have taken to planning vacations together. The past couple years, we rented cabins in a Jellystone campground in western Pennsylvania.

I'VE BEEN GONE long enough from rural Pennsylvania, with its green hills, soft trees, humidity, and narrow horizons to feel nostalgic for it now. I have limited vacation time, and I love to travel, and it makes me laugh that for two years in a row I willingly spent some of my precious days off at a buggy campground where diesel vehicles blasting cartoon theme songs passed by our dank cottage every ten minutes. But my daughter was awestruck by the

Yogi Bear characters that made scheduled showings around the campground. All three kids were overjoyed with each other, with the seventy-five-cent ice cream cones at the trading post, with the pool. In the evenings, my brother made the kids laugh uproariously. My father stepped back to allow him that role, to take his pleasure in looking on. The bonds of family. I balk at them but choose them. I was happy to be there.

One late afternoon my father and I found some time to sit alone together on the porch of the little cabin that was always in shade. It'd been ten years since I learned that Toshi had been arrested for sexual assault, and since my mother had told me my father had helped take Toshi away from Chiyo. Finally, I managed to ask about it: "Mom said something about you having helped Morris kidnap Toshi when he was little. She didn't remember any details. What was she referring to?"

The furrows in his face deepened, but he told me straightforwardly, if less fluidly than he would one of his usual yarns: Morris and Chiyo had already split up. My uncle was in Japan with the infant Haruna. Toshi was with his mother, not in New York City, as I had imagined, but in Indiana. Morris called my father and told him to drive down to Indiana and pick up Toshi, allegedly for a visit—that's what Chiyo believed, and my father did too. But when my father got Toshi back to Pennsylvania, my uncle told him to keep the child there until Morris got back weeks later. And my father obeyed. Toshi never lived with Chiyo again.

"She kept calling me at my apartment, and she was so confused. If she had been more savvy, she could have had me arrested for kidnapping," he said. "I had taken a child across state lines. What he had me do was very serious. And he never asked me, he told me what to do. He *demanded*. That's the way he was all our life." For a moment I sensed my father's return to his own beleaguered boyhood, to a younger brother bitter at being and used and tricked again. "Toshi was the same way. They both had that manner. They would demand things."

My father told me that Toshi had called him when he was arrested for child sex assault and said he needed help. My father had paid for his lawyer and his bail.

I felt a swell of outrage.

But my anger fizzled without catching fire. These new pieces of information didn't hold the same earth-scorching voltage as the earlier ones. I didn't challenge my father about his support of Toshi, not because I was too shaken and afraid to speak, but because I had found a weary acceptance. I'd already incorporated the idea that the story of my cousin was bigger than myself and that my father was implicated in it, that his concern expanded beyond my well-being. His thoughts were caught in old traps, different from those in which I found myself ensnared. When he thought of Toshi, he was reminded of his own mistakes and his brother's cruelties. I could see that he was offering me what he could. I had accepted that all parents make errors of judgment. And I was calmed and strengthened by my own ability to finally ask some questions, and to sit still for the answers. They were sad, and spoke of failures. But they didn't pound as ominously out in the air as the speculations did in my head.

"That's a tragic chapter in my life, and the one about which I have the most regrets," my father said solemnly, as the Yogi Bear Picnic Basket truck rumbled by. A couple of families sat on top, representing several generations. The parents were sunburned and big bellied, the grandmothers neat and clean, the towheaded kids bedecked in light-up jewelry purchased in anticipation of evening. People come to the park for their children. Sometimes they get so used to it they keep coming back after the kids are grown.

My father and I sat together in the woods in Pennsylvania, very close to where I grew up.

A WELL-REASONED ARGUMENT

uring the time when my intentions to write a memoir were firming, I went with three fellow writers to do a reading at the Prairie Lights bookstore in Iowa City. I'd just published a novel and was honored to be invited to read at such a legendary place, but during the long drive there I found myself questioning the endeavor. Was a seven-hour round trip to read to ten or twenty people and maybe sell a book or two worth the time and energy? My kids missed me when I was gone in the evening, and I'd been having trouble fitting in any writing around my full-time job as it was. I had to remind myself why I was going: Among the people who showed up might be someone who would really love my book, find the thing expressed that they'd had rattling around half-articulated in their own chest.

As it turns out, that person was not in the audience the evening I read at Prairie Lights. But I got a different kind of reward. The podium was placed in front of a shelf of books, and as I sat waiting for my turn at it, one of the face-out titles seemingly stood up and pointed at me: *The Trauma Myth: The Truth about the Sexual Abuse of Children, and Its Aftermath.* The phrase *trauma myth* struck a chord. The gap between my experience of sexual abuse and the cultural reading of it was one of the things that I was compelled to explore and had never heard discussed. Is that what this book was going to address? After the reading, I fielded questions from someone in the crowd who was interested in my experience with writing programs. I wanted to help the woman, but I was as aware of the book as I would have been years earlier of a hot guy making eyes at me across the room while I stood in a conversational knot I couldn't get out of. There was the same tension between where my attention must appear directed and where it was drawn. Finally, I got *The Trauma Myth* in hand and opened it to the jacket copy: "On a rainy night some years ago, a man presented himself at the office of Susan Clancy, a researcher in psychology at Harvard University. He'd seen an ad in the newspaper, calling for adults who were victims of sexual abuse as children. He was one. And he had a question: He hadn't experienced the abuse as traumatically as everyone thought he would—his emotions were complicated. He wanted to know if that made him strange."

Yes! I thought. *His emotions were complicated.* Another person approached me with questions about how to maintain a writing life, but this time I was able to focus, because I had the book in my hand and I knew I was going home with it. After so many years skimming books on sexual abuse before putting them back on the shelf, I had finally found one I wanted to purchase.

MY EXCITEMENT was borne out. Susan Clancy's book presents experiences closer to my own than anything else I had read or heard on the topic. Her thesis is that the dominant view that child sex abuse is traumatic for the child at the time of the occurrence—the assumption that forms the basis for most public education about and treatment of abuse— is not based on evidence, and that in reality, most children do not experience trauma when the abuse occurs but come to it later as they realize what happened to them. Based on her interviews with hundreds of people, she posits that it's this very shift in understanding that's at the root of victims' psychological disturbance—that victims come to feel guilt and shame because they didn't recognize the revolting nature of what they participated in, that they didn't try to stop it and may have enjoyed some aspects of it. She states that because most adults feel so shocked and sickened when they hear about child sex abuse, they have been blind to the way a child's developing conception of sex, adults, and society affects his or her perceptions. When survivors learn that society views sexual contact between children and adults as horrific, they might come to wonder whether there's something especially abnormal about them because they didn't react as if it were when it occurred. They will see few or no signs that their response is actually nearly as common as molestation itself. Certainly, that was true for me.

I connected with much of her subjects' testimony. Like many of the people she interviewed, my understanding of and reaction to my sexual abuse has altered over time, and I've struggled to make meaning of it. I've felt uncertainty about whether I was a "real" victim of abuse, about whether what happened to me was all that bad. I've felt awkward and suspicious in the face of the dominant narratives about sexual abuse and recovery, and I've wondered if there was something abnormal about my response—to the abuse when it occurred as well as the way I've dealt with it since. And, since learning about Toshi's subsequent crimes, I've felt a huge amount of guilt for not telling about the abuse, for not stopping it, not stopping him. Rationally I know not to, but the emotion is there.

I gulped the book down, greedy for all the accounts with which to compare my own experience. I was especially interested in hearing about when the victims' switch in their understanding of events occurred, and how they dealt with that. For many of them, puberty was the time when they realized that they had been manipulated into taboo acts. I recalled the afternoon I disclosed that I'd been molested to Heather Moosier, the difference between what I thought I was offering—a sex story to keep up with hers—and how she responded, as if I'd told of something somber and criminal. By that time I'd already developed the fledgling sense that Toshi had tricked me, but Heather's response was my first nudge toward realizing just how outside the main his and my interactions had been, how disgustedly others might view them.

I came upon a passage in *The Trauma Myth* that brought me back to the breakdown precipitated by my visit to my cousin's house in D.C.: "Research shows that people have a tendency to let current psychological states bias their memories of past events. The worse you feel at the time someone asks you about a previous event in your life, the worse you remember the past event to be." My cousin's questions about my parents had already opened wounds I'd been trying to ignore about their divorce and my dad's realigned priorities. No wonder I had freaked out so dramatically, burst forth with the news about what Toshi had done to me, and then cried about it for weeks. And then there was the time in New Mexico when I learned that Toshi was accused of abuse against another little girl: Of course I had responded violently. I had just become a parent myself. I was sleep-deprived, wracked with anxiety about my crying child, quivering under my responsibility to him.

How satisfying to be able to chart my experience with the help of a well-argued, well-written book. For the first time, I saw the appeal of fitting into an interpretation. If Clancy had interviewed me, though, I wonder what part of the transcript would have made it into *The Trauma Myth*.

I have no idea how many times Toshi came to me in the months that he lived with us—Ten? Twenty? Thirty? More? If I had walked into Clancy's office and been asked to describe my overall experience with molestation, the feelings of confusion and the wheedling and negotiation that took place in my bed would have been the things I'd have mentioned right away, because the occasions that featured them happened first and most often. That dynamic is what I think of when I conjure the experience of being molested. But an outlier instance exists, too. The time in bright daylight when I lay sick with fever and was plainly, baldly victimized and knew it, even if I didn't understand sex.

In the midst of her research, Clancy asked an expert on psychological trauma why her subjects were not remembering the sexual abuse as traumatic. He answered easily: It was because of dissociation, he said, the mental response to psychological or physical pain that allows people to separate their mind from their body and distance themselves from painful events. Clancy's tone expresses some scorn for this explanation: "In short . . . the victims who spoke to me did not report any trauma because the abuse was so traumatic that they had disassociated it when it was happening and as a consequence could not remember it correctly."

But I do not scoff at the concept of disassociating. I recall doing it quite vividly on that one afternoon, can feel my mind slip away from the bed like the wet pulp of a champagne grape sucked from its velvety skin. I did it other times too, when the transaction had been on its surface more consensual but the feelings were too strange for me to lie still for otherwise. However, my very recollection seems to place me in another kind of experience-canceling loop, since according to the expert, disassociation is not something to be remembered but something that prevents remembering.

One of the arguments Clancy poses is that whereas theories based on the trauma model posit that the more extreme the abuse the worse and more long lasting the psychological consequences to the victim, the exact opposite may be true. According to *The Trauma Myth*, because victims who went along with abuse are likely to blame themselves when they are forced to reconceptualize the past from a more informed perspective, their psychological damage may be greater than that of children who were overwhelmed with force or violence. "The less traumatic sexual abuse was when it happened, the more betrayal, guilt, isolation, and shame victims will feel and the more psychological distress and dysfunction victims may experience in the aftermath," Clancy writes. But the switch feels a little easy, a bit too convenient to her claim.

While I recognize that I've used the worst memory of Toshi as a solid piece of evidence of wrongdoing at times when the rest of the terrain has seemed muddled, it's not been the memory easiest to move beyond. When I think about that one day, my eyes still get wet and hot, and I want to throw up, and my muscles ache from unreleased adrenaline. When I think about the other times, when the molestation was less invasive and I could refuse some aspects or give at least surface-level acquiescence, I mostly just get squirmy and queasy.

I don't fit in any one schema. I bet that's the truth about many of us. Marriage is unknowable from the outside, they say. So may be the dynamic between the child abused and the abuser, even if some aspects of the scripts are common. At the end of her book, Clancy herself seems to recognize this. In her conclusion, she outlines her argument and issues concrete calls to action to the psychological community and society at large: Protect children by increasing adult awareness of the actual facts around molestation, acknowledge the confusion children might feel around sexual issues, believe victims even when it's inconvenient, press charges. But her last paragraph is addressed to survivors. "Do not wait to be asked," she says. "Speak out . . . you have nothing to be ashamed of, demand to be listened to . . . There are millions of you . . . The end of sexual abuse may ultimately come not from the hands of professionals or the institutions they serve but from the victims themselves."

This seemed grandiose, and even to be putting too much pressure on those who have already suffered—the *end* of abuse?—but *The Trauma Myth* did stoke my confidence in my own project. Repeatedly, Clancy's research subjects had mentioned how isolated they felt because their experience of sex abuse didn't match the cultural narratives they'd heard about it. Again and again, they told her they were participating in her study after never having disclosed the abuse before because they wanted to offer their experience in case it could help someone else.

"WHAT'S GOING TO MAKE your story different from all the other ones like this?" a writer friend asked me when I told him what I was working on. Then he mentioned to me that he'd recently embarked on a memoir-type project that featured his youthful obsession with baseball statistics.

Behind my friend's question I perceived the common view that sexual abuse was an overdone topic, predicable and maudlin, not the stuff of literature. I'd been affected by this assumption, too. But when I tried to recall recent books about the ambiguity felt in the wake of molestation, I couldn't think of any. Did they exist? If so, I wanted to read them. I didn't see them as precluding my own, I saw these hypothetical books as partners in a dialogue I'd been waiting to have. I wanted to leave behind the flat prose of psychology texts and frame my own experience, imprint it with my own cadences. And in so doing I hoped to connect across the page with others and ease the isolation I'd felt about this part of my life.

I t's springtime, it's springtime. Once again it's springtime. I have been living in this house with my husband for seven years, longer than I've lived anywhere since leaving my parents' home twenty-seven years ago. Long enough to know some things: the crocuses come up first, and then the grape hyacinths.

Don't mistake me for a gardener. For a good part of the year, my flower beds bring out my shame. Unbeautiful and untended, they symbolize my fears of not measuring up—I have neither the time to improve them myself nor the money to hire out the job. They are a chance for beauty being forgone. They are a sign of domestic obligation that I want both to master and shun. They reveal that I don't quite belong to the artists creating visual pleasure nor to this lovely community my husband and I have consciously rooted our family in.

But in the early spring, I don't think like this. The bulbs I purchased on sale in late November and sometimes December and shunted into the ground willy-nilly, with little consideration or skill, mostly do come up. Their green shoots reinforce my love of my own heartbeat. After the crocuses and the grape hyacinths come the bright yellow daffodils, and next the bi-color kind, and then the tulips, and the few regular, sweet-smelling hyacinths the squirrels haven't gotten to. Last year I added a puny strand of forsythia to the side of the house, and it bloomed! After a dormant year because I pruned them at the wrong time, this year the lilacs I planted did too, and the wedding bush that was here when we bought the house overflowed, pushing through the porch railings and expanding over the uneven bricks of the bed border. Around the time that bush starts popping, our whole town smells of flowers, and I can't believe I get to live here. Pear blossoms canopy the streets and lilacs festoon the yards. It's a wonderland. Though our plot of land doesn't look as good as many, I remind myself that I'm contributing, I'm adding a little more to the riot each year. As the wedding bush fades the mystery bush to the right of our porch steps starts to flower; I'd almost given it up for dead a few seasons ago, but an aggressive pruning has brought it back better than ever. Pruning: an act that can foil blooms or encourage them to flourish. There's a science to it, I know, but I live with it unknown.

The past few springtimes, a robin has built its nest on a ledge of our front porch, in view of the living room window, and our family has followed the proceedings with joy and trepidation. We watch the bird tuck in sticks and fluff and spruce things up. One day we notice her sitting there long, and we guess that she's laying or has laid. When she finally ventures off, my tall husband stands on tiptoe and holds his phone above the nest to take a picture so we can count what's in there—three blue oblongs this time. How many will make it? We've seen mothers fly away from their eggs and never come back. We've seen azure shells crushed and yellow yolk smeared on our gray porch floor. My husband has surreptitiously removed the body of a dead bird baby fallen or pushed from the nest so that the children won't see it and gain proof of life's cruelties. But this year, live chicks emerge from all the eggs. We watch the mama feed them—out and back, out and back, the babies' beaks always open, the gape bigger than their heads. How hard the mama works! If we come out to sit on the porch she'll often fly to the branch of the tree and squawk and squawk. To scare us off? To reassure her children that she's there to keep them safe? We watch the chicks grow—so fast! From wobbly heads peeking just above the nest's rim to chests puffed and wings flapping,

flapping, bodies jostling for space and gaining strength, red feathers starting to poke through the spotted down on their breasts. One Sunday, on our way to my daughter's first ballet recital, we all happen to step onto the porch at the moment the last chick stands on the edge of the nest and—floof! Flap flap flap!—takes flight all the way to ground beneath the neighbor's hedge. It's a breathtaking wonder. But my daughter is worried.

"Pick her up, Daddy! Pick her up and bring her home!"

"She's gone, sweetie," Anthony says so tenderly. "She's too big for the nest now. But her mama knows where she is. Look, see her mama up there? She'll make sure her chick is all right."

And off we go to see my daughter in her first dance. The symbolism is too easy and ridiculous, I know, but I'm not making this up.

SPRINGTIME, when both of my children were born.

MY DAUGHTER has just turned five. She is brave, strong, and dramatic. She is pushing farther, acting out, pushing farther, acting out. She wants to swing on the monkey swing next door, which dangles from a tree set in between the sidewalk and the curb, and none of us are available to go outside or even be in the front room. "I can go by myself," she says. Our street is neighborly but well trafficked, and the notion comes to me with a pop: It's too easy for someone to snatch her. The thought stuns me with dread, even though I know the statistic, that the chance of this happening is infinitesimal, that she's a thousand times more likely to be harmed by someone we all know well and who we invite into our home. In reading about the prevention of sexual abuse, I've been reminded repeatedly how unhelpful is our tendency to overprotect for things that are almost never going to occur. And I believe in independence. Anthony and I confer in a few mumbled sentences. "Okay," we say. "But before you go out, we want to remind you about stranger danger." We tell her not to talk to anyone she doesn't know. Not to get in a car with anyone. That if anyone stops and approaches her, she's to yell loudly. Almost never happens is not the same as never happens, after all, but we don't want to organize our life around that.

She decides to stay on the front porch instead, and I feel both glad and sad. I probably handled that all wrong. But look at her. So tall. So strong. So sure. So wary. She has a mean death glare. She has a lot of confidence. She has a will of iron. My baby bird. My baby bear. My little wolf cub. We might give each other a hard time, but in the world I think she's going to be okay.

MY SON has just turned twelve. He has a girlfriend. Not a stand-in for the idea of one, but a girl that he knows well and likes as a friend as well as romantically. They've kissed. It's a strange pleasure to see him moved to make sweetheart gestures, to get her little gifts and anticipate their monthly anniversaries. I stand on the porch and watch him walk or skateboard off, to meet her or his other friends, to go to rehearsal or a lesson or out to lunch or to the movies. The town is his oyster, now. He's discovered the pleasure of corner stores as I did in junior high, sneaks quarters from my purse or Anthony's stash for bubble gum and chips. "That's stealing!" I tell him aghast, remembering that I did the same, picturing the covered ceramic box where my dad kept his change in the basement room that became his study after Toshi moved out.

I shiver with fear at the potential for my son's heart to break, hope there will be no peer pressure for him or his girlfriend to move forward more quickly on the sexual game field than they might be ready for. Hope that nothing dangerous or horrible happens to him in this realm or another. A new sullenness now descends on him at times, even as tears still spring to his eyes quickly in the face of frustration or nervousness, and sometimes overflow. But he remains so generally friendly and outgoing. "Hi Jeff," he calls out to our neighbor as he boards past. "Hi Karen!" he shouts to our family friend as she waits at an intersection. I'm reminded that when he was little, the street people in our old neighborhood knew him by name and exchanged greetings with him. None of the four of us quite has the temperament of my father—who wasn't perfectly equanimous either, of course, during the toughest years of childrearing—but with regards to how he greets strangers, my son comes close. It makes me so glad to see it, even as I hold my breath for him. How wonderful to greet humanity with such optimism, to have no reasons not to, or to overlook them even if you do.

MY FATHER comes in for a visit. My mother comes for longer stretches, often structured around times we need her help with childcare, but my father comes more often and his visits are a treat. He takes us to the circus. He takes us out for sushi. He makes a point to designate some time for the two of us, and he takes me out to lunch.

We talk about our writing projects. I know he follows me online and reads the essays and interviews I publish, and I've been dropping breadcrumbs in them, mentions of child sexual abuse and my own history with it, but in our conversations I've remained vague about the topic of my memoir. My obfuscation seems cowardly at this point, and I'm ready to come out with it.

"I'm writing about what happened with Toshi," I say, "and how my view of it has changed over time."

"I gathered that," he says carefully. Over the years he's been consistently enthusiastic about the pieces I've written on sex work, sex abuse, my sex life, and rape, and I haven't tried to shield him from them—we've been more fellow writers than traditionally father-daughter in this regard—but my sexual assault cuts closer to home.

"I think we write about what we can't talk about," a writer friend said to me once, and the statement rings true. But now I am talking. I mention to my father some of the trepidations I've been working through the last couple years: how I didn't want to infringe on the privacy of bystanders who were part of my story but are living their own, and how I didn't want to silence myself, either. I try to explain why I feel compelled by this difficult subject matter: that though I didn't necessarily view the molestation as a dramatic or totalizing experience, it's never sat right with me, it's never fully come into focus through any of the various lenses through which I've tried to view it. I want to make sense of it.

"Part of what I want to explore is the complexity of the situation," I say. "It tends to be looked at only one way, as this horror show, and my experience was a lot more nuanced than that. Among other things, I have some empathy for Toshi."

"I don't say this to excuse anything, but he didn't have an easy time of it," my dad says. "Morris was so abusive. He used to hit him. I mean, he'd really punch him out."

"That's awful." For a moment I imagine receiving the force of that kind of blow. I am grateful once again for my luck in the father lottery. "I'm trying to

be fair," I say, "and to show restraint, but there's hard stuff in the manuscript about the family."

"Well, of course that's the case," he says. "I trust you. I know you'll do a good job."

My heart lifts at hearing those words, even though my father's trust is something I've always known I had. I trust him, too. We may let each other down in ways, he might wince at what I write, I might be hurt by his responses, we might communicate none of this perfectly—but our trust and love will still be there.

WE'RE AT A RESTAURANT that is not far from my home, but my father can no longer walk the distance. At the end of our lunch, I call my husband and coordinate with him to come pick my dad up. I wave at both men as they take off in the car. Then I walk back toward my office, relieved by my solitude. My step is light. I'm part of a family, part of a current. I'm one of the millions who've been sexually abused, yes, that too. I'm also myself, with my own story to tell, on my own. I'm conscious of the cool spring air around my bare neck as I cross the street.

The following organizations and institutions were consulted in the writing of this book:

Administration for Children & Families
American Academy of Child & Adolescent Psychiatry
American Civil Liberties Union
American Psychological Association
Bureau of Justice Statistics
Casa for Children
Crimes Against Children Research Center
Center for Disease Control and Prevention
Center for Judicial Excellence
Darkness to Light
Kids Count
National Center for Children in Poverty
National Child Traumatic Stress Network
National Children's Advocacy Center

National Domestic Violence Hotline
National Institute of Justice
Social Work Today
United States Department of Justice

ACKNOWLEDGMENTS

A writer always needs support, and I felt particularly hungry for it as I wrestled with this personally difficult subject matter. I'm fortunate to have received the help of so many.

Thank you to Gina Frangello, whose positive influence on my writing life cannot be overstated. She was the first person to whom I sketched the concept for this memoir, and her keen interest and understanding motivated me to pursue it through to the end.

Thank you to my writing group, which includes Gina as well as Emily Tedrow, Rachel DeWoskin, Dika Lam, Thea Goodman, and Rebecca Makkai. These smart, kind, talented women were my first readers and provided invaluable insights and the companionship of fellow travelers.

Thank you to Rob Roberge, Claire Dederer, Emily Rapp, Megan Stielstra, and Claire Bidwell Smith, authors whose early support for my project meant all the more because of the admiration I have for their own work.

I'm grateful for the time and information given to me by Lenore Zion, an author and psychologist with specialization in sexual pathology. Her knowledge about pedophilia helped me untangle confusion that arose during my research. Any mistakes I've made on the subject are mine.

Thank you to the many writers with whom I've conversed, commiserated, or celebrated online, especially Laura Bogart, Sarah Einstein, and Amy Monticello.

Thank you to Sari Wilson and Martha Bayne, wonderful readers and people with whom I've been sharing ideas since college. I'm more appreciative of their friendship each year.

I'm enormously grateful for my agent Alice Tasman as well as Tara Hart at Jean V. Naggar Literary Agency, who showed great dedication to this project over the long haul.

Thank you to my editor Naomi Huffman, whose close, smart attention to my manuscript made it much stronger, and to Catherine Eves for her hard work on the book's behalf, as well as to the rest of the Curbside Splendor team.

I wrote very few of these pages in my own home. Thank you to those who lent me theirs for spells: Gina Frangello and David Walthour, Cie and David Bond, Amy Davis and Lee Nagan, and Sandy DeBernardi. I'm also grateful for the quiet spaces provided by The Writer's Workspace, run by Amy Davis; Creative Coworking, run by Angela Valavanis; and the Evanston Public Library. Getting to these places was made easier thanks to friends and neighbors who've cared for my daughter, especially Jenn Gerard, Nehad El Gamal, and Karen and Kirby Girolami Callam.

Thank you to my soul sister Brenna Williams for the friendship that helped shape who I am, and to the bird goddess Valeria Ricketts who's flown the American coop but remains in my heart.

I'm grateful to my parents, Joan Zolbrod and Paul Zolbrod, for their love and open-mindedness, which made my world bigger and brighter than it could have been. My father has been especially generous in his encouragement and faith in the writing of this book. During my entire upbringing, he was working on a book of his own, and I have read the dedication to our family in it so many times its cadences have penetrated my bones. I think of it now when I thank my husband Mark, my son Tillio, and my daughter Lilli. They have put up with my writing-related moodiness, distraction, and disappearances for years, and have been there to dance, wrestle, and laugh with me when I return. I love them to my very core. This book couldn't have been written without the perspective they've given me.

ZOE ZOLBROD's work has appeared in *Salon*, *The Nervous Breakdown*, *The Weeklings*, and *The Rumpus*, where she serves as Sunday co-editor. Her debut novel *Currency* won a 2010 Nobbie Award and received an honorable mention by Friends of American Writers. Zolbrod lives in Evanston, Illinois, with her husband and children.

"Half romance, half meditation on global affairs, *Juventud* portrays how the past can affect the present and how memory can be fallible."

—FOREWORD REVIEWS

Curbside ✶ Splendor

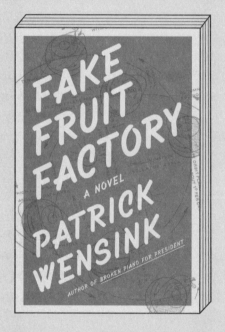

Curbside ✹ *Splendor*

CHICAGO INDEPENDENT PUBLISHING

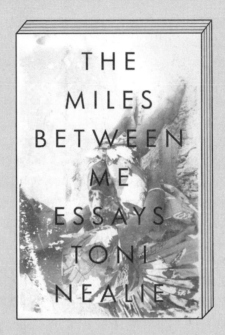

THE
MILES
BETWEEN
ME
ESSAYS
TONI
NEALIE

"With warmth, curiosity, and lyrical intelligence,
Nealie keenly parses the human reverberations
of dispersal, unraveling, and arrival."

—PEGGY SHINNER,
AUTHOR OF *YOU FEEL SO MORTAL*